Click

Click

WHEN WE KNEW
WE WERE FEMINISTS

—

Edited by Courtney E. Martin
and J. Courtney Sullivan

SEAL PRESS

Click
When We Knew We Were Feminists
Copyright © 2010 by Courtney E. Martin and J. Courtney Sullivan

Published by
Seal Press
A Member of the Perseus Books Group
1700 Fourth Street
Berkeley, California 94710

Library of Congress Cataloging-in-Publication Data

Click : when we knew we were feminists / [compiled] by Courtney E.
Martin and J. Courtney Sullivan.
       p. cm.
  ISBN 978-1-58005-285-6
  1. Feminists–Biography. 2. Women authors–Biography. I. Martin,
Courtney E. II. Sullivan, J. Courtney.
  HQ1123.C55 2010
  305.42092'2–dc22
  [B]
                                        2009025525

Cover design by Ann Weinstock
Interior design by Lucie Ericksen
Printed in the United States of America
Distributed by Publishers Group West

For our fathers,
Ronald M. Martin
and
Eugene F. Sullivan Jr.

—

Courtney E. Martin and
J. Courtney Sullivan

CONTENTS

click

click

INTRODUCTION

Click. The flipping of a switch. The cartoon bulb flashing on overhead. The light suddenly illuminating the darkness. This romantic notion that ideas and identity are formed in one lightning-strike moment used to be the purview of old, white guys—Greek philosopher Plato, whose metaphor for enlightenment involved escaping creepy shadows in a cave, and inventors, like Alexander Graham Bell and Eli Whitney, who swore their earth-shattering insights happened suddenly and by accident once upon a time.

Jane O'Reilly reclaimed the click for the ladies in her 1971 *Ms.* magazine cover story entitled "The Housewife's Moment of Truth." Appearing in the inaugural issue, it opened with a group of women lying on the floor in Aspen, "floating free and uneasy on the indoor/outdoor carpet, eyes closed, being led through the first phase of a Workshop in Approaching Unisexuality."

The women "recognize the click! of recognition, that parenthesis of truth around a little thing that completes the puzzle of reality in women's minds—the moment that brings

click

a gleam to our eyes and means the revolution has begun." The backdrop of O'Reilly's story is distinctly early '70s, and the realizations that occur on that (no doubt, shag) carpet seem somewhat fixed in time, too. One by one, the women O'Reilly describes realize that they can no longer tolerate the sexism all around. She writes:

In Houston, Texas, a friend of mine stood and watched her husband step over a pile of toys on the stairs, put there to be carried up. "Why can't you get this stuff put away?" he mumbled. Click! "You have two hands," she said, turning away.

Last summer I got a letter, from a man who wrote: "I do not agree with your last article, and I am canceling my wife's subscription." The next day I got a letter from his wife saying, "I am not cancelling my subscription." Click!

Last August, I was on a boat leaving an island in Maine. Two families were with me, and the mothers were discussing the troubles of cleaning up after a rental summer. "Bob cleaned up the bathroom for me, didn't you honey?" she confided, gratefully patting her husband's knee. "Well, what the hell, it's vacation," he said, fondly. The two women looked at each other, and the queerest change came over their faces. "I got up at six this morning to make the sandwiches for the trip home from this 'vacation,'" the first one said. "So I wonder why I've thanked him at least six times for cleaning the bathroom?" Click! Click!

We began our own conversation about click moments in a definitively modern context—a mass email sent to several of our feminist friends. J. Courtney Sullivan was in the process of writing her novel, *Commencement*, and needed an idea for the feminist "aha moment" of one of her characters. She emailed a group of women and asked, "What was the moment that made you a feminist? Was there one person, event, book, or idea that made it happen?" The responses came in fast and furious. Some were predictable (reading Katie Roiphe, joining the campus women's center, having a sexual assault experience) and some were anything but (seeing Jennifer Baumgardner wearing fishnet stockings, or Alissa Quart falling in love with a war correspondent). Our click moments were distinctly different from those Second Wavers in O'Reilly's essay.

Responses to our email chain included:

"We were reading The Great Gatsby *in high school English, and I came across this line: 'That's the best thing a girl can be in this world, a beautiful little fool.' I felt enraged, but none of my classmates even seemed to notice."*

"Was it The Feminine Mystique? *Catharine MacKinnon? Attending Smith and realizing that I needed to do more with my life in order to honor the legacy of the women who came before me? Weeping for prostitutes in Amsterdam? My 'Come to Jesus' moment was kind of like a slow buildup over time that culminated with me waking up one morning a RAGING feminist—although I was definitely a minor one from the start."*

"At a rainy Take Back The Night rally my first year of college . . . I looked around at the women on every side, and thought about how strange it was that I'd ended up here, given my conservative Republican upbringing. I realized that if I don't identify as a feminist, no one really does."

"One movie: Girls Town. *Amazing."*

Courtney E. Martin, inspired by the range and surprising nature of many of the answers, suggested that we ask more young feminists that same question. We wanted to collage together a picture of contemporary young feminists—often invisible to mainstream media entirely and sometimes maligned by their own foremothers for supposedly misinterpreting the movement they've inherited. We wanted to discover what it is that still brings a diversity of young people to try on the feminist label despite the obvious risks. And we wanted to represent what we saw as the awesome breadth of feminist baptisms in the modern age. Back in the day, the most common path toward a feminist identity was getting dragged to a meeting by a friend or reading a feminist book. Today, a girl Googles Jessica Simpson in her living room in Dubuque and stumbles on a feminist analysis of Simpson's creepy dad on a blog—suddenly, she's wondering if she might be a feminist, too.

Click is a collection of essays on the catalytic moments when twenty-eight women and one man in their teens, twenties, and thirties were disoriented by sexism and found their way to feminism. From protest marches to marching bands, Anita Hill to Patricia Hill Collins, late night stand-up to purity pledges, ADHD to engineering school, Barbie dolls to Sleater-Kinney—these essays depict a definitively modern version of feminism, reshaped and reinvigorated by the daughters of the '80s and '90s. Their stories and backgrounds are diverse, but they share a passion for feminism that proves the movement is as strong as ever.

In these pages, you will hear from some of the most beloved and controversial voices in contemporary feminism—including Jessica Valenti, Jennifer Baumgardner, Amy Richards, and Rebecca Traister—as well as some fresh new perspectives from writers like Sophie Pollitt-Cohen, the whip-smart daughter of Katha Pollitt; the youngest Feministing editor, Miriam Zoila Pérez; and eighteen-year-old Nellie Beckett, who says, "Buying a pair of sturdy, sensible black boots was a classic feminist milestone . . . I developed a confident stride that carried me farther, faster, more powerfully than I dreamed possible. One day, I put a pair of flats back on. I had to mince down the street with that booty-shaking hobble that so many girls learn after they've forgotten how to run and jump. Some advice, girls: Once you get a decent pair of shoes, there's no going back."

The inspirational moments, people, and events that draw young women to feminism are everywhere—but this generation of the movement faces many challenges that others never did. First off, we face the question, is feminism still necessary? Some of our contributors speak to the idea of always supporting women's rights, yet not initially feeling the need to ally themselves with a formal movement. American women in their twenties and thirties have benefited immensely from inroads made by our mothers and grandmothers, and a by-product of this is that many young people see feminism as outdated and unnecessary. Here, we reveal what changes their minds.

In some circles, despite progress made by feminists a generation ago, it's still difficult or controversial for young women to claim the feminist label. How then do they find their way to it? Some of us grew up in conservative homes and neighborhoods, but used the Internet to bridge the geographical gaps between like-minded young women and ourselves. Others, unlike Second Wavers, were raised by self-identified feminists; for these women, the quest is often characterized by trying to find their own version of feminism—separate from their mothers' consciousness raising groups and Gloria Steinem books. (Jessica Valenti writes: "She is the reason I am who I am. Ironically, it was also her strength that spelled my reticence to the feminist label. It was all just too scary. To call myself a feminist was to identify with my mother.")

Feminism is alive and thriving, a movement with a rich history that constantly gets reshaped and redefined. Our book owes a debt of gratitude to Jane O'Reilly's 1971 essay, though it is different in so many ways. That's fitting, really, because our generation of feminists owes a debt of gratitude to hers, despite the changes of the last thirty years. Our contributors write as if in constant, fearless dialogue with the movements and the

click

meanings that have been inscribed by the women who came before. They don't ignore the past, but honor it, all the while looking ahead.

Almost forty years ago O'Reilly wrote, "One little click turns on a thousand others." We offer her—and you—this collection as a gracious acknowledgment of the lights that led the way and an illumination of those to come.

— *J. Courtney Sullivan and Courtney E. Martin*

I'M GONNA WASH THAT KING
RIGHT OUT OF MY HAIR

Elisa Albert

———

It was the spring of 1989 at Temple Emanuel Community
Day School of Beverly Hills (motto: "Living Judaism!").

Purim is the raucous Jewish holiday commemorating the
victory of the ancient Persian Jews over an evil government
plot to exterminate them. As relayed in the Book of Esther
(a.k.a. the Megillah) it went down something like this: King
Ahasuerus, presiding over a drunken gathering one night,
sends for his queen, Vashti, to come and "entertain" the party.
This is understood to mean, in the vernacular, *show us yer tits.*
Vashti says screw that, I'm not your bitch, don't tell me what
to do. The king promptly throws her out and looks through
his harem for a replacement bride. He finds and falls madly
in love with the beautiful/virtuous Esther, who, having been
so advised by her beloved uncle Mordechai, does not reveal

her Jewish identity. The real trouble begins when Mordechai refuses to bow down to the king's hateful adviser Haman and a personal vendetta is born. Haman plots to destroy all the Jews in the kingdom. The king says sure, whatever, do what you want, I don't care about those weird-ass Jews. Mordechai impresses upon now-Queen Esther the importance of putting a stop to this plot. Esther fasts for three days, soul-searching, and finally goes before her husband the king to reveal her identity and plead for the sparing of the Jews. The king's dick proves more influential than either his personal bigotry or his highest adviser, so the Jews are saved, Haman is sent to his death, and, a few thousand years later, we motley fifth- and sixth-graders pull out all the stops on a musical revue spectacular.

We all wanted to be Esther, of course. The heroic, beautiful, self-sacrificing beloved of the king. The ingenue savior of the Jews. And such a nice girl, to boot. So thin from all that fasting! She was going to get to wear a dirndl and sing a re-lyricized "My Favorite Things." Second choice would've been to play a member of Esther's harem, biblical pole-dancers who got to wear these very sexy getups—veils, MC Hammer pants, exposed midriffs, sequins: very Persia Britney Spears. (Eleven-year-old girls in midriff-baring harem costumes: ah, good old Jewish day school.) The king, surrounded by his minions and ogling a parade of bachelorettes, was given to breaking the fourth wall, winking at the audience, and exclaiming, à la Mel Brooks, "It's good to be king!"

I was ambivalent, at best, about having been cast as Vashti. The shrew. The cast-off first wife. A mere footnote to the story of Esther's bravery and the salvation of the Jewish people. My costume was a modest polyester gown. My big number was "I'm Gonna Wash That King Right Out of My Hair," and I was last seen protesting the harem procession, pacing back and forth downstage with a large sign that read WOMEN UNITE!

The harem girls got all the attention, not to mention the good outfits and camaraderie. They giggled and shrieked, primped and preened, traded lipstick and headdresses. Vashti walked her picket line alone, back and forth, a feminist army of one.

Sure, it wasn't the most nuanced portrayal of feminist values, but lo and behold, the audience ate it up. They positively roared. On the VHS I scavenged from a musty box in my mother's basement, you can see a relieved and astounded smile creeping over my face, replacing the enraged, playacted protest and alienation. And something crucial sparked in my prepubescent brain: Sometimes the pretty, virtuous little princess is a freaking snooze. Meek Esther was revealed to have a somewhat underdeveloped stage presence and proved quite unmemorable. But everyone found Vashti—in serious eyeliner and tiara, shouting down Biblical gender paradigms—hilarious. ("Women, Unite! Women, Unite! Women, Unite!") I already had a reputation for being tough and loud and something of a handful (to, um, euphemize), and now it seemed I'd found an acceptable outlet. On *stage*, no less.

How fun and exciting (and attention-getting) to be protesting and shouting and refusing. How very much more interesting to go against the grain. And wait a second, *yeah!* Why the hell was it okay for the king to demand sexual favors from his queen and then unceremoniously dump her if she didn't feel like putting out for him? I was too young to fully get the situation—though I had, by then, discovered and memorized my older brothers' extensive hardcore porn stash—but the injustice of the situation seemed clear, and I ran with it.

My friend Raquel, in a nice bit of gender-play, was cast as Haman, and before being sent to the gallows in the show's final act, delivered a truly heartrending performance of "Don't Cry for Me, Shushan City."

Our director, an Israeli woman named Nili with a frosted perm and lots of blue eye shadow, was exacting and visionary. I wonder now about her artistic goals: Did she aspire to an experimental off-Broadway career? Did she go home at night and complain to her theater friends about the bunch of over-privileged elementary school brats in this ridiculous Purim musical?

Thanks to the miracles of Facebook, I can today account for about 75 percent of my talented costars. But not Esther, because I can't for the life of me remember her name.

It was, by all accounts, a triumphant show. Thereafter, though, I was confused to have earned myself a reputation, and had become the target of a fair amount of teasing: Hey Elisa, are you a *feminist*? Hey Elisa, women belong in the kitchen! Hey Elisa, are you going to get married and have lots of babies like women should? Hey Elisa, are you a lesbian? A good many peers, and even adults, in my life seemed to find it cute to bait the grade school feminist. I found myself embroiled in verbal spats about my burgeoning identity, forced to defend ideas I didn't yet understand. Despite the fact that I was utterly without the tools to properly argue my as-yet-unarticulated case, it was clear to me that something was off: This "feminism" thing got me into creepy one-sided arguments with grownups.

My elderly great uncle tersely advised me, ostensibly in response to my fifth-grade feminist harlotry, to "keep my legs crossed." Another relative liked to mock me with statements like "Women shouldn't be doctors," just to laugh while I sputtered furiously in disagreement. It pissed me off long before I could fully understand what was going on.

Some years passed before Grace Paley and Naomi Wolf and Jean Kilbourne and Gloria Steinem and Ani DiFranco and Vivian Gornick and Susanna Kaysen and Andrea Dworkin kindled the spark of a complex adult feminism, but I'm convinced that my embrace of the above-mentioned hinged on already having identified—in that stubborn, childish, attention-hungry, dinner-party-delighting way—with Vashti. Her refusal to degrade herself for the entertainment of her shmucky husband and his shmucky friends, her dignity in the face of being dumped and cast aside, her sadly lacking place in the Old Testament, singular refuser of ancient gender paradigms.

The Megillah doesn't give us much detail about what happened to Vashti, but it's likely she was put to death at the king's insistence. I'm not very observant these days, but every Purim—a holiday on which it's a mitzvah to get so drunk you can't tell the difference between Haman and Mordechai!—I toast her spirit, and my fellow players in that long-ago Shushan spectacular, for helping me begin to see what resistance is all about.

ONE IS SILVER AND THE OTHER'S GOLD

Jennifer Baumgardner

When I was a little girl, I played with Barbies religiously. They weren't my only pastime—I also loved the *Carol Burnett Show* in reruns, singing Barbra Streisand songs at the top of my lungs, and roller-skating. But the summer of 1979, Barbie reigned supreme. I played Barbies every day with my next-door neighbor Missy, a green-eyed ten-year-old (I was nine), who was the daughter of the pastor at United Methodist. I had Malibu Barbie (who had straight hair with bangs, a tan, and suggestive lighter lines of paint where her bikini had blocked out the sun) and another Barbie with knee-length wavy hair and an opulent pink evening gown (Vegas Barbie? Barbie Dream Girl?). Each day I would drag my Barbies, Barbie furnishings, Barbie car, and Barbie clothing over to Missy's. We established a narrative: The Barbies were in college and living in dorms and were always getting ready to go out on dates. They were, while possibly not gay, bi-curious—in the sense that I often positioned them to lie on top of each other naked. Missy had a Ken, and that came to no good end. Pretty soon Malibu Barbie was pregnant and needed an abortion. She got pregnant many times and always chose to have an abortion. After all, she was in college, bisexual, and popular, and abortion was legal.

I was raised steeped in a brew, however weak at times, of feminist values and culture. It was a function of era (the '70s) more than location (Fargo, North Dakota) or sensibility. During the Vietnam War protests and drug experiments of the 1960s, my parents were struggling young marrieds, scraping by while Dad finished med school, and then we spent five years on army bases while my dad did his military service. Still, my mother read Ms. My father wanted everything for his three daughters that sons would have gotten. We talked about abortion and gay rights at the dinner table—the whole family was for both. My childhood was invisibly, but perceptibly, enhanced by Title IX, access to birth control and abortion, and a Free to Be . . . You and Me attitude. But these gifts from the women's liberation movement weren't clicks, as made famous by Jane O'Reilly's 1971 "The Housewife's Moment of Truth"— they didn't unlock a feminist consciousness but rather enabled me to live a pretty unencumbered life without having to be part of a movement.

By college, 1988 to 1992, I was a passionate, if conflicted, feminist. I danced suggestively at frat parties in miniskirts with my friends while yelling, "Don't look at me!" at any oglers. I read the big authors: Millett, Firestone, hooks, Dworkin, Anzaldua . . . still nothing had occurred that could be called a "click." It was more like I was channeling clicks from another generation, nodding my head in agreement with "all men benefit from sexism" and "abortion on demand without apology!" I quoted from brilliant, outraged manifestos written by women who were raised in the 1950s, women for whom feminism landed like a meteor in their lives, initiating cataclysmic change in their carefully laid-out existences. I laughed ruefully about my preconsciousness nine-year-old self who played with Barbies, those pink, plastic, acceptable versions of womanhood.

By age twenty-one, the ideas of feminism thrilled me. The power the movement had put in so many women's hands was palpable to me. Its recent history was so glamorous and righteous; I was sad I hadn't been around for it. Jealous, even, of these revolutionized housewives and women who had been excluded from jobs, college, the military, leadership, and drinking at McSorley's Ale House. Why couldn't I be one of the women so angry about the high-dose pill (which caused blood clots and strokes and had been unethically tested on women in Puerto Rico with no attempt at informed consent) that I broke up the Senate Pill Hearings in 1970? By the time I was on the Pill, the hormones were at a mere fraction of the previous dose, safe for most intents and purposes.

But later, at the magazine where I worked after college, I got my click. It came not from desperately defying the housework my husband didn't help me do (I was unmarried and dating a girl), nor from learning that men in my office were paid more for the same work (I worked at Ms. magazine; there were no men). My click came from having an ally—a peer raised in much the same brew as I had been—who could reflect back to me what I was experiencing as a feminist raised *after* the Second Wave. If not for her, would I have continued recognizing feminism only if it looked and sounded like the Second Wave? Would I have continued to pile on to my own generation, agreeing with sentences like, "young women are so much less radical" and "so much less pro-choice" and "there are no young leaders"?

The ally was Amy, also born in 1970, though in a different kind of family than mine. She was raised by a young single mom, had never met her father, and had attended boarding school and Barnard—a somewhat common trajectory in New York City, but exotic to my Midwestern perceptions. I worked at Ms. magazine in the editorial offices, total peon job; Amy worked down the hall in Gloria Steinem's office.

At first, our interest in one another was social—two young colleagues, one new to the city, going out for a drink or to hear a band or dance at Nell's. But within a few months, we began talking shop: She would tell me about the younger activists she had met at the women's conference in Beijing or through her foundation, Third Wave, which at the time was basically Amy and a recipe file box with names of a few hundred donors and members. I would share my increasingly confident belief that women who were creating—not just critiquing—culture were the new generation of feminist leaders, the dearth of whom was so bemoaned at meetings we attended. Through Ms. (and my own initiative), I was meeting writers, musicians, and activists like Kathleen Hanna, Christina Kelly, Nomy Lamm, Ani DiFranco, Debbie Stoller, and Farai Chideya—women my age who were feminist and responding to their own era.

Those first heady conversations prompted an independent and accurate assessment of my own world and generation, its problems and potential solutions. Rather than my continuous repetition (and romanticizing) of feminist truths that came before me, I began to look in the mirror and see myself as important to feminism as the women who had come before me. I believe what I went through was entirely natural. When you are becoming radicalized, you gravitate to recognizably radical spaces. I felt I was a feminist but wasn't totally secure in what that might mean in my life. Therefore, I pretended to have Andrea Dworkin's life—or at least her perceptions, which were, of course, born of her personal and generational experiences.

At times, this new ability to see my own generation and myself as powerful and relevant felt like a betrayal of—or at least a conflict with—the Second Wave. I saw that social justice has a natural evolution to it. The '60s were a Big Bang. Abortion was illegal, contraception was illegal, black people were actively barred from rights of citizenship and living with dignity—or even living. To be gay or trans was to live in secret or face constant ridicule and prejudice. Women were hostages to a single stray sperm, allowed to be educated without a chance to apply this education in meaningful work. People protested their exclusion and oppression—they kicked open doors, they demanded to be let in.

But that way of being activist is less germane today, when exclusion is not the primary oppression. The activism of today is subtler, intersectional, individual, and sensitive. It requires listening as much as, if not more than, speaking out. It is the activism of inhabiting a space once the door has been kicked open, warming up the chilly atmosphere, creating the infrastructure for a healthy social environment.

I now lecture widely across the country. I've visited more than 250 schools, and at every school there is this anxiety that students today are too apathetic, that they are not angry enough about the wars, about abortion rights, about capitalism. When I was in college, I felt that anxiety and made the exact same indictment of my generation—not being angry enough—a direct comparison with the '60s. But I've come to realize that the job of each generation is to make sense of its own era—to understand what is needed now, when some past issues of oppression are not so in-your-face. To acknowledge that I am living a far more socially free and empowered life than my mother could have imagined at my age. I want to thank her and her generation for that groundwork, but more importantly I want to commit to inhabiting the rooms they helped to open up, and not continue banging loudly on a door that is unlocked.

Identifying that distinction between my generation's feminism and that of the Second Wave was a critical step in seeing what truly ties the eras, generations, waves (whatever you want to call it) of feminism together. It's this: It's a relationship with an ally that enables you to inhabit your feminism. The women of the 1960s and 1970s talked at kitchen tables, held CR meetings, formed countless groups, but the main thing they did was reflect back each other's experiences and call them, not just valid, but political.

One day in 1998, when Amy and I were in the middle of writing our first book together, we were struggling with our resistance to some earnest, feminist magazine targeted at girls. It might have been *New Moon;* it might have been *Teen Voices.* Something about it felt inauthentic to young girls today and imposed from another era—that whole aping of '70s feminism we felt encouraged to do early in our consciousness. Then we began to talk about Barbie. It took a while to jog my memory, but I recalled how much fun I had imagining adult life via that doll—and how much my Barbie was expressing the changes wrought by feminism, from sexual freedom to legal abortion. Meanwhile, Amy recalled that she would take photos of her Barbies, as if they were her older siblings, filling out her female-only family of two. "I liked Barbie," said Amy, decisively. "She was sort of a friend."

"Yes," I said and sent up to the gods of feminism a silent word of thanks for this ally with whom I reliably, and powerfully, clicked.

∽⊚∾

Seventeen Years of Ridicule: A Young Feminist's Polemic

Nellie Beckett

———

Click: the honks when I walk down the street.

Click: the snickers of my high school classmates when I speak up.

Click: the screech of misogynist lyrics.

Click: the laughs at sexist jokes.

Click: the sickening thud in the pit of my stomach when I walk home alone at night.

I am seventeen years old, and I've been a feminist as long as I can remember. Though I can't discern a particular "click" in my memory, perhaps it was when I was born at home and bestowed my mother's last name because my parents wanted to subvert the patriarchal naming system. Perhaps it was at the age of two, when I expressed a preference for blocks and toy trucks instead of Barbie dolls. Perhaps it's just the experience of growing up female in a misogynistic society. Fortunately, I've had the privilege of a supportive home environment. Ever since I can remember, my feminist mother has taught me to analyze the implicit messages in Cinderella, speak out against misogyny, and stick up for myself and others. My politics are also shaped by my father, who taught me to cook, read me Pippi Longstocking, and took me to the 2004 March for Women's Lives. Personally, I'd like to think that I have played an integral role in shaping the feminist beliefs of my two fabulous younger sisters.

Still, it's not easy growing up female, especially when you're teased from a young age for having a loud mouth and strong opinions. The label *feminist* memorably resonated in second grade, when I sat transfixed through an entire documentary on the Seneca Falls Convention. When I read *Reviving Ophelia* at the age of ten, I realized that I couldn't make the transition from confident kid to depressed, troubled teenager like so many of the girls profiled in the book. The more books I read and the more injustice and sexism I saw, the more feminism made sense. Thus my career as a raging, self-identified radical feminist was born.

Feminism instantly clicked because it was a way of seeing the world that made sense, respected and aligned with my perceptions of society. The more I learned about the movement, the more power I felt. Identifying as a feminist has fortunately inspired both mundane and life-changing decisions.

I've learned to speak powerfully, ridding an upward inflection at the end of sentences in favor of making definitive statements. It makes defending strong opinions and unpopular positions much easier.

Buying a pair of sturdy, sensible black boots was a classic feminist milestone inspired by Anastasia Higginbotham's fantastic essay in *Listen Up*. I developed a confident stride that carried me farther, faster, more powerfully than I dreamed possible. One day, I put a pair of flats back on. I had to mince down the street with that booty-shaking hobble that so many girls learn after they've forgotten how to run and jump. Some advice, girls: Once you get a decent pair of shoes, there's no going back.

Getting a short haircut may have been a superficial choice, but it still felt like one less societal restraint had been lifted. One of the happiest days of my life was when I walked home with a short cut, more confident than I had ever felt before. Now the shouts I hear from car windows are "dyke" rather than "baby." I take the intended insult as a term of pride.

Coming out was terrifying, exhilarating, liberating—a defining experience that proved that the personal is indeed political.

This is not to say that all feminists are short-haired, hairy-legged, sensibly shod lesbians. In fact, I've found that feminist defenders often waste half their rhetoric dispelling this tired stereotype. Feminists come in all shapes, colors, and genders, and it's about time that our diversity is recognized in the main-stream. If there's a movement whose image shouldn't be the top priority, it's feminism.

Luckily, my undying activism does have a fun side. With a feminist consciousness, it is much more rewarding to stay up reading radical feminist polemics rather than watching TV that's hell-bent on convincing my demographic of our collec-tive deformities. Writing zines is more useful than waxing my legs, clinic defense is better than the mall, meeting my feminist icons is more exhilarating than just about anything.

Though I have an unwavering loyalty to the basic tenets of feminism, I struggle with its boundaries every day. At what point do you draw the line between being sex positive versus sexist? Can we consider pro-lifers to be feminists? How can the feminist movement include people who identify beyond the confining categories of man and woman? These vexing binary questions are enough to make me want to retreat to one of the almost-extinct lesbian feminist communes and stick to the hard-line radical feminist rhetoric that sounds so appealing in theory but is so difficult to make a reality. Unfortunately, separatism is awfully constricting when the definitions of everything in our world are blurred. Inclusiveness is the only way that this ever-shifting movement is going to progress.

However, personal definitions of feminism will always be extremely complex. Being a feminist means making my own choices, but it also means supporting the choices that women in my life make. I'm a feminist for my mother, who chose to stay home with her kids and was criticized for doing so. She's now applying to be a lawyer. Despite her excellent credentials, law firms seem to think that fifteen years as a stay-at-home mom don't qualify as "real work." I'm a feminist for all my friends coming out, getting together, breaking up, finding themselves, struggling with body image and the nagging feeling that they will never be good enough. I'm a feminist for my grandmother, a breast cancer survivor and former debutante, who spends an hour a day on makeup, yet self-identifies as a feminist. I'm a feminist for my cousin, the single teenage mom of a beautiful baby girl. I'm a feminist for my baby-sitting charge, who at five years old adores Disney Princess movies, Barbie, and the color pink. I make sure to tell her that she's strong and smart, as well as pretty. I'm a feminist for humans of every gender who are beaten, raped, teased, ignored, excluded, discriminated against, silent, and shamed.

I'll continue to be a loud and proud feminist for so many reasons. Because women are still paid 75 cents to a man's dollar, because one out of three women is a victim of sexual violence, even because I can't walk down one block in my neighborhood without being catcalled or harassed. I could list the statistics and anecdotes all day, and even then there are so many people who refuse to acknowledge privilege and oppression of all kinds.

I've had to explain to stupefied peers countless times: Feminism is not just about equal pay. My generation is young, foolish, and utterly dependent on technology. They are blissfully unaware and often, it seems, worrisomely inactive, if not willfully ignorant. This is not to dismiss the wonderful work of youth activists everywhere, but to highlight the common misconception that our struggle is over.

I try not to make the classic teenage assumption that my own experiences are universal. I know they are not. This is why I am a feminist.

Still, I'm young and I make mistakes. Despite devoting extensive amounts of my short life to feminist education and activism, I have so much to learn and so much to accomplish. I don't know it all, nor do I pretend to. My ideology may seem naive one day. I am not the first person to discover and recite these feminist sentiments, to experience "clicks," nor, do I hope, the last.

Click: A protestor at the clinic where I volunteer as an escort: "Honey, you shouldn't be here killing babies. Why don't you go to the mall and buy some makeup?"

Click: An essay prompt in English class: "Women use feminism as an excuse to complain about their lives. Defend, challenge, or qualify this statement."

Click: A quote from a buzzed-about pop singer: "I think it's great to be a sexy, beautiful woman who can fuck her man after she makes him dinner. There's a stigma around feminism that's a little bit man-hating, and I don't promote hatred, ever."

Feminist "clicks" come so fast that I can't differentiate between them. So many clicks every day, all the time, and the noise becomes a galvanizing buzz that wakes me up. The buzz turns into righteous anger, fueling my joyous existence and action in a movement that has enough room, enough heart, enough power and potential for everyone. So, I offer up paraphrased lyrics of Riot Grrrl goddess Kathleen Hanna to my own generation: I dare you to do what you want and be who you are. You do have rights, you know.

∽◈∾

CROSS-STITCH AND SOAP OPERAS
FOLLOWING FOOTBALL

Jordan Berg Powers

In 1957, when women weren't getting an equal opportunity to compete in sports and for athletic scholarships, Sheila Berg got multiple offers from universities around the country to compete in basketball, gymnastics, and swimming. She led the way for Title IX, showing that women could compete and help build universities' sports programs.

When a community needed young hearts to lead a mobilization for equal rights, that same young college student, Sheila Berg, got onto a bus and traveled to Mississippi and Alabama. Attacked by police and dogs, she stood firm demanding that her fellow Black Americans be allowed to register to vote.

And in 1980, when her nation needed her, she joined the U.S. Air Force. Even though the military banned her from fulfilling her dream of becoming a pilot, she became one of the first female jet engine mechanics. She knew that if women were going to be allowed to fulfill their dreams, she needed to push the boundaries of what society perceived women capable of.

Sheila Berg led without ever seeing it as her duty as a woman or a Black American. In fact, she told me, her son, "I just had stuff I wanted to do, and I didn't believe anyone could stand in my way."

Leading was nothing new. Sheila had the example of her mother, who was one of the first Black women in America to get, not only a college education, but a master's degree as well. My grandmother grew up in a shack in the rural South, sharing one room with her mother, a freed slave, and seven siblings.

I grew up in a feminist household led by amazing feminist women who refused to be identified as feminists. I was encouraged to see everyone as equal, taught to be as inspired by Sojourner Truth as I was by Dr. Martin Luther King, as indebted to Stanton and fellow Seneca Falls dignitaries as I was to Washington and Adams. Despite all of this, when I asked about feminism my inquiry was met with a flood of four-letter words and commentary about how white women were out of touch with reality, especially the reality of Black women's lives.

I kept searching—unable to square the lessons I received, both explicit and implicit from a female-led household, with the historical and philosophical information I was learning about progressive movements in America. I was learning how to see society through a feminist lens—deconstruct the inequalities I was seeing around me and reimagine the world as a more just place. And yet it was these strong women, my mother and her mother, who were vocally opposed to what they perceived feminism to be.

As a growing boy, though unaware of the political implications of the things I took for granted, I still had a sense of the imbalance inherent in male privilege. I noticed little things, like how my female friends were often last to be picked in gym class or on the basketball court at recess. I tried to encourage my female friends to speak up when my male friends dominated a conversation.

I was an emerging feminist unable to claim the label. I still had to reconcile my mother's concept of feminism with what I was perceiving on a daily basis. To complicate the issue, my interests and passions didn't square with societal concepts of masculinity. My MC Lyte tape got stolen because it was seen as "pussy" music. My love of sewing and cooking were discouraged by a home economics teacher who didn't want to foster those passions in a boy. She tried to encourage my love of sports instead. My sexuality was questioned because I treated women as friends, with empathy and respect—behavior my own mother had instilled in me. I had to come to the understanding that, even as my mother hated the box into which she perceived that "feminists" tried to fit her, she was acculturating me into a similarly gender-stereotyped box.

I had to put my mother's understanding of the feminist movement in historical context. My mother's perception of feminism was born out of her struggles for acceptance in a white, male-dominated society in the 1970s and 1980s. Back then she was trying to be a Black, professional mother and wife, but on her own terms. For my mother, feminism meant giving up being a woman. She saw and still sees feminism as the desire to reach equality by masculinizing womanhood—that the way to be equal is to leave her femininity behind—to be equal to a man meant to be a man. To her, feminism meant a restriction on what it meant to be a woman, in terms of dress and actions, and thus no better than the men who thought that as a woman, she couldn't carry a heavy toolbox and fix an Air Force C-130 Jet Engine. She wanted to be a "girly girl" working in social work on weekdays and fixing complex, heavy jet engines when her nation called.

Worse, she felt, that the dominant feminist culture required her to choose being a woman (in those narrow terms) over her blackness, rendering her race invisible. She worried that feminists saw being a woman as one oppression and racism another. For her, feminism was not relevant because it didn't adequately address her world as a Black woman.

Of course, that was the same sort of box my mother was trying to put me into. While she was so proud that I played football and basketball, she questioned my masculinity when I would come home from practice and watch soap operas, while finishing a cross-stitch. I had to play down my compassion for people's emotions, my desire for fairness, my love of color coordination, because they weren't "manly enough" for Mom.

Strange as it sounds, the drips and drops of consciousness culminated for me in a pre-Christmas *Late Night with Conan O'Brien*. . . . The show that particular evening featured Martha Stewart, a confident, self-made woman who found success mixing homemade crafts, food, and ideas with a keen business sense to create an empire. My perception before ever hearing her, reading her magazines or books, or consuming any of her craft ideas was one of a cold woman who was somehow less important because she made her money helping people beautify their homes. O'Brien, playing on this cultural stereotype, made comedic hay out of getting her to drink beer—"a lower-class liquor."

I was profoundly disturbed by the way that this self-made woman was dehumanized. It clicked. I made a connection between the devaluing of my mother that I saw every day—from upscale stores that wouldn't serve her to the looks she received while carrying her toolkit to fix jet engines for the Air Force—to none other than Martha Stewart. They were both put into a similarly restrictive box.

Why were my mother and Martha Stewart "bitches" for being strong women? We put women into restrictive boxes and unfairly beat them down (figuratively and, all too often, literally), should they dare to try and break out of this cell.

But the suffering caused by these restrictions is not limited to women. Just as my mother was confined by the box society put her into and frustrated with the box she perceived feminists were putting her into, she confined me with unfair expectations based on gender stereotypes. Rather than embracing who I was, she wished for me to match society's ideals about traditional masculinity.

Martha Stewart isn't less of a woman because she runs a successful business empire, just as she isn't less of a homemaker for liking beer. She is all these wonderful things together—a multifaceted person. Just as my mom is both a dedicated wife and mother *and* can lift a sixty-pound toolkit to fix a C-130's jet engine. Just as I love watching sports *and* ironing clothes.

Feminism is the fundamental and, some would say, danger-ous belief that women are, and should be treated as, equals. Feminism is about empowering women to be whatever they want to be, to break walls that oppress and stagnate women.

And when you put one gender into a box, you create a companion box for the other gender. So while women suffer disproportionately, men are also cheated by the boxes they have to fit into—boxes that tell us that we need to be strong by being cold and obtuse, domineering and thoughtless in our relationships with women, unable to understand the complex-ity of feelings—let alone have them. Society dictates that men are to be no more than animalistic simpletons; the bigger we are, the less evolved we must be (an assumption that, as a large black man, I know all too well).

It is at that intersection of privilege and oppression that feminism helped to clarify my once-obfuscated view of the world, enabling me to deconstruct the injustices around me and take off the blinders we're all taught to wear. That was my true click moment—the moment I connected the boxes. We re-create these boxes subtly and unconsciously. "We are all recovering sexists," former vice presidential candidate

click

Rosa Clemente once said. Women and men, comedians and my mother—we're all complicit in re-creating the oppressive patriarchal society.

Feminism opened up my narrow worldview to allow me to be critical of my surroundings and ask the important questions, like "Why do my feminist role models not like feminism?" I was able to reconcile their resistance, understandably born in the past, with my own enthusiasm today. I stand on their shoulders with the values they entrusted to me and proudly identify as a feminist and do feminist work.

My mother, I have grown to understand, is my feminist role model even if she may never call herself a feminist.

❧

KILLING IN THE NAME OF

Elizabeth Chiles Shelburne

For the men in my family, one's eleventh birthday was a momentous occasion. At that age, the state of Tennessee considered a child old enough to hold a firearm to his shoulder, squeeze the trigger, and kill an animal. Girls weren't excluded from this rite in any strict, statutory respect, but, in practice, eleven was just another birthday for the female children of Tennessee. As the state goes, the family goes. Pictures of my older brother holding his first deer, shot when he was eleven, adorned our house—the deer's blood smeared down his forehead and nose in a testosterone-fueled rite of passage.

My father was a small-town lawyer who sometimes got paid in old trucks or dental visits. He remains one of the best-read people I've ever met, as well as a devoted hunter. In the style of Southern gentlemen of old, he is Atticus Finch and Larry the Cable Guy all rolled into one charming package. He'd grown up hunting and continues to hunt every year—and not just deer. He also hunts quail, turkey, pheasant, and even elk. We had grown up eating the fruits of his hobby, and my brothers could barely wait for their chance to join him.

What was never imagined was that the girls might want to come along. My sister, four years older than me, had allowed her chance to pass blithely by, and the men thought I'd do the same. My younger brother was already included in eager conversations about his first hunt. It was assumed that he would hunt. And I would not.

Growing up in a family with four kids, you become acutely aware of what is or is not *yours*. "Mine. Don't Steal" might well be the motto for my life, much to the dismay of my husband (mine, don't steal)—a man who is committed to the principles of sharing, particularly of food. In this hunting discussion, the men had taken my answer for granted, without bothering to ask. They had stolen MY opportunity. I was furious.

"I want to go hunting," I said at the next conversation about my younger brother's impending eligibility to go kill stuff, a few months before my eleventh birthday. My brothers laughed so hard they fell out of their chairs. It was preposterous, inconceivable, that I, a girl, would ask to mar their man time.

"You can't do that!" they cried, united against the affront to their masculinity.

"I want to," I said. My father, who, unlike my brothers, understood the need for sensitivity where the feelings of women were concerned, merely nodded his head.

"You know, there is a class you have to take," he said. The hunter safety course. I knew I had to pass it to get a license.

"And the guns are heavy. You'll have to lift it on your own," he said. I nodded again. If they thought my little brother could do it in a year or two, then I *would* be strong enough, come hell or high water.

"And there will be blood, Elizabeth," my father said. I rolled my eyes at that one and stuck out my chin defiantly.

The fury I felt from being told I couldn't do something just because I was a girl was like none I'd ever experienced in my ten years on earth. I was a girl on a mission. I would go hunting. I would show those boys that girls could do anything they could do, even if a deer had to die to prove it.

"I want to do it. I want to go hunting," I said.

The boys kept up their mockery for months, but my dad soon realized that I was serious. He found a class, looked up the days for the youth hunt, and was as encouraging to me as he had been for my older brother, albeit in a quieter fashion.

The hunter safety classes were held over several evenings in the local high school. The first night, I walked into the room and ran into a veritable wall of camouflage, as if at any moment these men and boys expected to be called upon to brave the wilds of our company town in pursuit of animals in need of killing. I wore jeans and a T-shirt and got more than a few looks that plainly wondered if I'd gotten lost on the way to the sewing class that was also offered that night.

We spent the nights going over basic safety lessons designed to keep us from killing ourselves and others. We learned how to recognize a loaded weapon, how to engage and disengage the safety, how to climb into and out of a tree stand (a platform up in the trees, about fifteen feet off the ground) without blowing our heads off, along with some vague hunter ethics and training in marksmanship. The last consisted of teaching us, via a cardboard cutout of a deer, that the best place to shoot one was right behind the deer's shoulder. A bullet in that spot will go through a deer's heart, killing it instantly.

There was also a live practice day out on the shooting range. Of the twenty or so odd guns my father owned at the time, he brought a Winchester .30-30 rifle, the same one I'd be using the day of my hunt. I'd gone out to the range before, but there had never been so much on the line.

45

click

My first shot was atrocious—only God knows where that one went. I lowered the butt of the gun to the ground and clasped my right shoulder. I felt the gun's kick reverberating through my shoulder to the top of my head down to my waist. For a four-foot, seven-inch girl, a rifle packs a powerful punch.

As I gripped my shoulder, aching with a pain I'd never before felt, I felt a trickle of fear. What if I was wrong? What if a girl, this girl, couldn't do it? What had I gotten myself into?

Then my brothers' faces, midlaugh, came to mind. My stomach flashed hot with anger, and I gritted my teeth and hoisted the gun to my shoulder again. I was ready. The kick hurt even worse this time, but I didn't let my grip slip for a minute. The bullet sliced through the target a couple hundred yards away, a perfect shot.

The day of the hunt finally arrived. At 4:00 AM, to hide my scent from the deer, I took a shower with no-scent soap and dressed in thick long johns, all freshly laundered in no-scent soap. I could hear my brothers snoring as my dad made coffee downstairs. We packed the guns into the back of our old Suburban and stowed the two thermoses, one loaded with coffee for my dad, the other full of my mom's hot chocolate for me.

We stopped at Hardee's for breakfast. Full of camo-dressed grizzled old men and their sons and grandsons, the restaurant was the only place open early enough to accommodate the hunters' need to get into the woods before the sun rose and the deer emerged from the undergrowth where they'd bedded down the night before. I yawned over my biscuits and gravy and smiled shyly at the boys, all of whom looked as nervous as I felt.

In the dark, we drove out on the highway to the next county. I was too nervous to talk, and too afraid to say something stupid or wrong on this, the most important of mornings. I wondered what my brother had talked about on the drive to his first hunt. Was there some prehunt bloodlust conversation that I, as a girl, had no idea how to initiate?

We pulled onto a gravel road and puttered our way up, passing hundreds of maples tumbling down the hill toward the river, their branches empty, and the ground carpeted in the warm brown of rotting leaves. Dad had been hunting this spot for years now and knew exactly where to pull off. In the predawn chill, I pulled on my brother's hand-me-down bibs, rolled them up at the ankles, and tucked them into my boots and socks. As a last step, I applied one of the world's foulest-smelling substances, red-fox pee, to my boots—more attempts to camouflage our very human scent. Finally, we were ready.

My dad walked down the shoulder of the road and stood beside the barbed wire fence. I followed him, my heart starting to pound louder and louder. We scooted underneath the fence and set off into the woods. After twenty minutes of walking, Dad stopped and pointed up. There, fifteen feet off the ground, was the tree stand.

Dad motioned for me to go up first. I climbed up the pieces of wood he'd nailed to the tree's trunk, a handmade ladder, perfectly proportioned for him, but spaced a little widely for an eleven-year-old girl. Just as I was starting to get scared, I pushed my head through the little cut-out in the platform and hauled myself up. Dad followed. We sat on plastic milk crates, arranged boxes of bullets, thermoses, deer grunt, and a knife on the floor around us, and settled in to wait.

And wait.

In my months of preparation, I'd learned Tennessee's hunting laws, how to shoot, and how to tell my brothers to shove it in eleven-year-old language. What I hadn't prepared myself for was the activity that composes the bulk of hunting—freezing your ass off. My toes went numb first, then my fingers, and then my core. But I was tough. I wasn't going to wimp out. I waited until I saw Dad take a sip of his coffee before I made a careful move to my own thermos. But the hot chocolate, as good as it was, just reminded me of all that I was missing by putting myself on this stupid mission—namely being asleep in a warm bed. As the sun rose around us, I found my head nodding over my gun.

Suddenly, there was a crack from the woods around us, a branch breaking under the weight of an animal. A few minutes later, a doe stepped out of the underbrush and began to delicately lip through the leaves, searching for the acorns underneath.

In the youth hunt, you are allowed to kill both bucks and does, and so my dad nodded at me, giving me the go-ahead. I wonder now if he would have done the same for my brother, or held his arm back when he lifted the gun, indicating he should wait for a buck to come through. I don't know. I do know that I didn't give it a second's thought. This was my deer.

I was no longer cold or numb as I lifted the rifle to my shoulder and took aim. I took a breath and slid the safety catch off with my thumb. I smiled nervously at my dad and then turned back to the deer, my face overtaken by a look of grim determination. This was it. This was my moment to stake my claim as the first female hunter in our family. I aimed for just behind the deer's shoulder, right where we'd been taught, and took a breath.

I squeezed the trigger. The shot rang out. The deer fell where she stood.

I burst into tears.

My dad, used to the whoops and hollers of my older brother, had no idea what to do with those tears. I knew this wasn't what I was supposed to do and tried to stop, but I couldn't help it.

"You did great, Elizabeth!" my dad said. "You got it. It was a great shot."

And still, I cried.

"What's wrong? It was perfect," he said, his face clouded with confusion and concern.

Perhaps this is the hazard of hunting with girls: We cry when we succeed. Or maybe it's just me.

Finally, I wiped my face with my glove, sniffed so loudly any deer within a two-mile vicinity heard it, and followed my dad down the ladder. By the time my feet hit the ground, I had papered over my guilt with excitement. I'd killed my first deer. I'd proved my brothers wrong. Dead wrong, in fact. If I'd embarrassed myself by crying, then so be it. They couldn't ignore the facts: Girls can hunt.

I skipped over to my deer and turned to face my father with a huge smile. "I'm going to call her Lucrenda," I said. The look on his face suggested that naming the dead animal wasn't a usual practice, but I didn't care. I had killed a deer to prove a point, and the least I could do was give her a name. I was like Sebastian in *The NeverEnding Story*, naming the princess.

It had been a perfect shot, right through her left shoulder blade. Her pink tongue stuck out slightly between her thin black lips. Full of excitement and pride, I stared down at my prize, watching as the cool wind dried the liquid that lubricated her eyes, the life literally fading from them.

I became a gun-toting, camo-wearing eleven-year-old feminist the day I decided that I was going to do exactly what men told me I could not. But in the days after my hunt, I couldn't stop thinking about Lucrenda. I had expected glee or at least satisfaction. But the look on my brothers' faces when I came home with Lucrenda didn't make me feel as good as I had thought it would.

That's the thing about proving a point—once done, you sometimes realize it wasn't worth much. In my pig-headed determination to show the boys that girls can do anything they can, I hadn't ever thought about whether it was something I *wanted* to do. I wanted to prove them wrong, but did I want to kill to do it?

The point I had really proved was that I had allowed myself to be defined by what the boys said I couldn't do, rather than by what I wanted to do.

I accompanied my little brother and dad on a hunt the next year, where I basked in the tepid sun over East Tennessee's rolling hills and drank hot chocolate. On my final hunt, the last time I've been in a tree stand, I did all the parts of hunting I liked, and none that I didn't. It was a perfect day.

~๑~

Empowerment in Soft Focus: Growing Up Female with ADHD

Li Sydney Cornfeld

———

Everyone knows the ADD stereotypes: unruly little boys with a penchant for punching whose parents get suckered by pharmaceutical companies, and spoiled prep school kids whose parents buy them extra time on the SAT. Fear of stigmatization kept me hiding in the girls' bathroom after standardized tests. And yes, it sometimes makes me reluctant to talk about disability, sexuality, and feminism even now, at age twenty-five. Yet I continue to believe the best way to break a stigma is to out yourself.

When I started school, my writing consisted of giant, scratchy capital letters. It's easy to giggle over the wild six-year-old scrawl in my old spiral journals, so huge that single words take up whole pages, until arriving at entries from my classmates: Despite an occasional misshaped letter, their legible writing is carefully balanced between the pale blue lines. I like to think now that my hard, huge words reflected the fury with which I tried to convey my ideas in a medium that didn't come easily. Thinking of words did—in conversation, I was always friendly and articulate—but the act of writing them down was extraordinarily difficult and took me a very long time. Sometimes it felt like I wrote slowly because my hands couldn't move as fast as my mind could think. Other times it felt like I just made connections at a slower pace, or at least in a different way than my peers did. "I've never had a student who thinks like your daughter," a junior high math teacher told my parents when I failed her course. She didn't mean it as a compliment.

My memories of my early school career are a blur of me sitting at a desk with everyone staring at me, realizing a teacher has called my name but not knowing if I'm meant to answer a question or read from a textbook. I was always the last kid to turn in class work and tests. Countless nights, I stayed up hours past my bedtime to finish my homework only to leave it at home the next day. These are telltale signals of a learning disability, and I was lucky to go to excellent schools with small student-teacher ratios, so why didn't I get a diagnosis until my junior year of high school?

My coping techniques were alarmingly textbook: When I forgot my homework or lost track of a class discussion, I would giggle and apologize profusely, so that my behavior seemed spacey or ditzy but not wildly irresponsible or indicative of a more serious problem. I might have been diagnosed sooner had I not picked up on the feminine practice of apologizing for myself. On the rare occasion that anyone suggested my parents take me to a specialist, they shied away from doing so out of fear that a label like LD (learning disabled) or ADHD (attention deficit hyperactivity disorder, sometimes called

ADD) would carry more repercussions than benefits, that I would be discriminated against.

Well-meaning teachers allowed me to bring home my incomplete class work and finish my tests at recess, and when I managed to complete my work, what I turned in was really good. Yet that shouldn't have affected my seeing a psychologist: A learning disability is not a synonym for stupid. The quality of my schoolwork shouldn't have mattered; the pace at which I completed it did. The high rate of girls with unrecognized learning disabilities is maddeningly reminiscent of other social realms in which women are rendered invisible. As in the case of so many sexist stereotypes, the cultural conception of ADHD as a problem of solely little boys—and the fact that girls' learning disabilities read as normal—damages everyone.

Teachers, and even clinicians, are often trained to recognize ADHD only as it presents in boys, who tend to have hyperactive type ADHD; inattentive type is more common in girls, which is perhaps partly why male diagnoses outnumber female diagnoses at a rate of three to one. Inattentive type is often more difficult to recognize: I was alternately described as spacey, disorganized, slow, a daydreamer. To be sure, I was— still am!—all of those things.

I am slow. Very slow. I'm not using slow euphemistically, to mean unintelligent, the way we say "special" when we mean "retarded" or "interesting" when we mean "unattractive." I mean that it actually takes me an inordinate amount of time to complete most cognitive tasks. Rather than manifesting itself in hyperactivity, inattentive type ADHD produces a sort of hyperfocus. "Attention Deficit" is something of a misnomer: Rather than lacking an ability to focus, I concentrate too intently. I become so engaged with a singular activity (reading a book, talking on the phone, watching a fly on the windowsill) that I lose focus on everything else.

click

Everyone experiences moments like that to a certain extent, which may be partly why some are hesitant to recognize inattentive type ADHD as a disorder. But while what I do is somewhat akin to becoming so engrossed in a terrific movie that you let the popcorn burn, the scope of my behavior is more chronic and more extreme. Take, for example, the day in third grade when a substitute teacher called my name and I lined up at the door, lunch box in hand. Only then did I realize that everyone was staring at me, and then we all erupted into giggles, though I wasn't quite sure why. It turned out the teacher had just been going around the room, checking to make sure she knew our names. We'd already been to lunch.

When I was finally given a diagnosis, a month shy of my seventeenth birthday, what my condition meant wasn't exactly news to me; I was intensely aware of my problems. Yet receiving a label for them felt more validating than I had imagined possible. I didn't realize how badly I'd wanted to be told there was a reason I was always the last student to turn in a paper, the kid who looked up confused at instructions given too quickly, who left the remote control inside the refrigerator. *You Mean I'm Not Lazy, Stupid, or Crazy?* the title of a popular guide to adult ADD by Kate Kelly and Peggy Ramundo, succinctly sums up the relief I felt at adopting the ADD label. Far from making me feel incompetent or stigmatized, as my parents feared it might, the diagnosis was my first big step toward empowerment.

An understanding that both the nature of my disability and the reason for its late diagnosis were related to my being female drew me to feminism. The parallels are plentiful. When I completed my AP U.S. history exam a full three hours after my classmates, I hid in the girls' bathroom so I wouldn't have to join my class in the middle of last period. It wasn't that I thought I didn't deserve my testing accommodations or that I felt guilty about receiving them, exactly. But I was afraid people would mistake my needing accommodations to make the test equal with my receiving extra time as some sort of perk—and that, if questioned, I wouldn't know how to explain it. I didn't yet have the vocabulary I needed, and in my head, "dude, why would anyone choose a six-hour test?" didn't seem to cut it. Any woman who has worried about, say, requesting maternity leave should have some idea of what that's like.

In college, I found the words to more fully engage in learning disability activism and feminist discourse and saw still more connections between the two. My understanding of feminism as a movement that strives to welcome diversity of both experience and thought falls right in line with LD/ADHD empowerment, which literally celebrates thinking differently. I know that historically feminism has struggled with incorporating perspectives of women (and men) of diverse classes, races, abilities, and experiences. I'm mindful of disability activist Judy Heumann's observation that when she's among feminists, "all they see is a wheelchair." I realize that to a large extent, an invisible disability like ADHD allows me to pass. But I see contemporary feminism as engaged in a more conscious effort to be inclusive, and to me, the essence of disability activism is wholly aimed at inclusion: creating points of access for people of different abilities to engage with one another.

Like members of lots of marginalized groups, as an ADD feminist I struggle with whether it's more useful to mimic dominant cultures (i.e., to try to think like a "normal" person and to copy patriarchal patterns, respectively) or to embrace worlds of difference on their own terms, whatever they may mean. Striking an appropriate balance of the two is different for different people, and I appreciate ongoing dialogues on the subject that exist within both groups. A question that sometimes arises in LD/ADHD conversations is whether or not the term *disability* is an appropriate description in the first place. Would *learning difference* be more inviting or less stigmatizing or simply more accurate? I sometimes respond that while all people learn differently, a disability is important as a marker of a condition. At the same time, I want to welcome those who are undiagnosed or who prefer not to have an official label. Still, proponents of using "learning difference" strike me as reminiscent of the "I'm-not-a-feminist-but" branch of feminism. Call it whatever you like: The beliefs are close enough. Personally, I need—want—both of the labels to identify with the communities they represent to me: smart, weird, fascinating peers with a vested interest in fighting for our own validity.

My relationship to labels, however, is nonetheless uneasy. I decided for a time that I was not just a case of missed diagnosis, but misdiagnosis. I wondered—still wonder—if rather than inattentive type ADHD I have a learning disability called an executive processing disorder. The conditions present similarly; neither diagnosis would lead to different accommodations in school. However, ADHD is sometimes classified not as a learning disability but as a behavioral disorder, and I resented the indication, however clinical, of anything inappropriate about my behavior, especially given that I never identified with the "H" of ADHD. When it occurred to me that describing myself as learning disabled was perhaps more accurate, I eagerly used the LD label because, I'm embarrassed to admit, it struck me as somehow more respectable. But these days, I no longer care much about which label is most applicable. The umbrella acronym LD/ADHD is all-encompassing; what matters is understanding how I think, capitalizing on my strengths, and compensating for my weaknesses.

It took me longer than it should have to realize that my relationship to the LD/ADHD acronym is much like my relationship to LGBTQ, an acronym more explicitly tied to feminism. At different points in my life, I've identified with most letters in both lists. Just as I've struggled to come to terms with my place inside LD/ADHD, I've agonized over which letters in the LGBTQ spectrum most accurately describe me and how that affects my relationships with friends, family, and the world around me. My inability to reach a solid conclusion regarding my place in either list frustrates me.

Ultimately I recognize both the LD/ADHD and LGBTQ acronyms for what they are: means of inclusion that recognize individual difference. I can't think of better examples of that feminist ideal, and I'm proud to be part of both acronyms, even as I'm perpetually uncertain of my place within them. I appreciate that feminism gives me not just a freedom to keep questioning but a framework within which to pose the questions. If the long trains of big capital letters occasionally feel a bit silly, calling myself a feminist never does.

Maybe I ought to have been smarter about acronyms all along. After all, big capital letters have made me simultaneously proud and embarrassed since my kindergarten notebooks and their brave, silly-looking words: capital letters that served as evidence of my struggles and as a form of self-expression. Writing them down was risky and confusing, difficult and liberating. I'm glad I did.

⟳

YOU ARE WHAT YOU WEAR

Anitra Cottledge

⌒

The year was 1997; it had been a little less than a year since I stood in my dorm room with my friends and watched the news about Tupac getting shot. Biggie still had "Mo Money, Mo Problems" months after his death. OJ had been acquitted a couple of years back, and a woman could luckily still find a nice shoe with a chunky heel. I was a sophomore in college at a predominantly white university hundreds of miles away from home, and I had one foot in and one foot out of a couple of different closets. One of my closets—the one with the big "F" engraved on the door—felt roomy and cramped all at the same time, like a loft space with books and CDs stacked in every available nook. It was 1997, and I was struggling with so many things: Should I double major in journalism and English? Who drank the last squidge of my apple juice? What should I do about this whole feminism thing?

The dilemma as I saw it: It's one thing to *be* a feminist;

it's a whole different kettle of fish to broadcast your feminist tendencies to the rest of the world. That's why, even though I loved volunteering at my campus women's center, even though that experience is the foundation for much of the work I do today, I honestly didn't want to wear my "Mizzou Feminism" T-shirt where just anyone could see it. And by "anyone," I mean the other black students in the food court, in the dorms, or in my classes. Somehow, I feared that if I proclaimed my feminism in the presence of other black folks, they would assume I was a lesbian (even though I was) who hated men (I didn't). As if being a lesbian wasn't enough, being accused of "being into some white shit," like feminism, would mean even further isolation from the other people who looked like me. If I wore that T-shirt around my peers, I feared I would be called out, and I just wasn't confident at that point in my ability to defend myself or my feminism.

When I finally gathered the courage to wear the shirt in public my junior year, it was A Moment for me. I don't think it was necessarily the moment when I realized I *was* a feminist. No, I had a different kind of "click" moment. Instead, it was one of the moments when I began to *claim* my burgeoning feminism. I started to contemplate what feminism could mean for me, and the way I thought about belonging and community. I hadn't yet discovered bell hooks, Audre Lorde, or Patricia Hill Collins, and I had no language to talk about feminism. What I understood, what I wanted, was a place to belong as I was sorting out who I was, and the way all of my identities—black, woman, lesbian, nerd, working class—could coexist. Finally being able to wear a T-shirt that labeled me as a feminist was probably the beginning of my struggle to integrate all of those identities into a whole that made sense to me.

But I'm getting ahead of myself and using language that's familiar to me now, but meant nothing to me then. In retrospect, I had been women-centered for a long time. In a way that was apart from my gender, or sexual orientation, women were the suns in my life, and everything else was just a satellite. No disrespect to the men in my family, but even then it was clear to me that the women were the ones who kept the family rotating on its axis. My paternal grandmother was the matriarch. I could talk to my mother about almost anything. And my aunt was my role model for pushing beyond the familiar. I credit my aunt with being the person who showed me another world was alive beyond my hometown. It was because of her that I knew what it was like to feel slightly out of breath from the thin air on Pikes Peak. Because of my aunt, I tried new food ("Oh my God, what is pad thai?") when I was still a teenager. All of those new experiences became my template for opening myself up to interesting and unfamiliar ideas and experiences I previously hadn't given myself permission to envision.

For better or worse, the conversations in my family were often initiated by the women and dominated by the women, and the decisions were made by the women. The women were the power brokers. Because of this dynamic, I knew, down to the marrow in my bones, that being a woman *mattered*. It had weight. I can't remember exactly what led me to the campus women's center, but I think I was subconsciously searching for another place where I could matter, a safe haven.

I found the safe haven before I found feminism proper. Gloria Steinem and the mythical bra-burning weren't even blips on my radar, when I found a group of welcoming, quirky, funky women who were doing their thing. Straight, lesbian, bi with piercings and tattoos, rail-thin, full-figured, this was a tribe of women who brought in videos of their childbirth experiences, who had heated conversations about body image, who curled up on the couches and watched *Say Anything* as a group and talked about how awesome Lloyd Dobler was, no matter their orientation.

I helped out with the center library and soaked it all up,

the discussions, the women, the energy. I stumbled upon books like *Unbearable Weight* and *The Feminine Mystique*. For a young woman from Detroit who had spent a lifetime feeling like a nerd (I was) and an outcast, it was such a relief to feel like I could just . . . be.

I did, however, notice that I was one of few black women—or women of color, in general—that frequented the center or worked there. I had no idea then that this was old news in feminist communities; I was completely unaware of the animosity that existed between some women of color and white women in the feminist movement.

The lack of melanin told me that something was wrong, though. If there weren't many black women jumping on the women's center/feminist bandwagon, that meant I couldn't talk about it with other black people. I couldn't be *that*. None of my other black friends talked about it. None of them were feminists (or at least, the rest of them were hiding like I was). So I became afraid—terrified, really—to talk about the issues that I was starting to care so much about and of the increasing amount of time I was spending in the women's center. Wear my "Mizzou Feminism" shirt out and about? Forget about it.

Something else was also taking shape around that time: anger. I felt rage like I had never before experienced. To this day, I call my sophomore and junior years my "militant days." I remember wanting to smack everyone, most especially the white people who seemed to feel entitled to everything, even the space on the sidewalk. Some moments were more blatant than others: a car full of white guys rolling around the bend, and a voice yelling out, "Nigger!" Drive-by racism.

Some were more subtle: White women in women's studies classes posed questions like, "Which came first, racism or patriarchy?" Because it's so easy to choose. The white women weren't the only ones who believed it was simple to choose. I was angry at the black folks, too, for what I perceived as their collective close-mindedness, for their insistence, too, that I choose which identity was more important: being black or being a woman.

This absence of the black feminist experience was everywhere, including the classroom. I had gotten my hands on bell hooks and *To Be Real* by Rebecca Walker by then, and I was on the warpath. I was angry that nobody was talking about my experience. I was furious that there were barely any women of color featured in my women's literature class, and that the professor had the nerve to spell Audre Lorde's name wrong! (Audre was my hero by then, and it was sacrilege as far as I was concerned not to take the time to spell her name right and recognize her contributions to the feminist canon.) I even had another English professor who didn't even know that Gwendolyn Brooks had died! I was so tired of Virginia Woolf and Anne Sexton and blah blah blah.

I said, "Fuck this," and built my own curriculum. *Black Macho and the Myth of the Superwoman?* Check. *Black Feminist Thought?* Got it. *This Bridge Called My Back?* Yes! I discovered a whole new universe inside of Alice Walker's *In Search of Our Mothers' Gardens.* I cast off feminism for the richer mantle of womanism for a while.

Consistent with the tricky nature of memory, I don't know what particular passage from what specific book, what special moment changed things for me. I didn't write down in my journal the exact day I started wearing the "Mizzou Feminism" shirt to the bookstore, to class, to the dining hall, consequences be damned. I just know that it was some time in those angry, questioning days when wearing the shirt became secondary to finding and shaping a feminism that fit who I was and reflected back to me my experiences and the experiences of the women in my family and the women that I knew. As I started to discover the various feminisms, wearing the "Mizzou Feminism" shirt became an act of defiance. It was open challenge: I dare you to tell me that this word, this movement, doesn't belong to me.

That challenge has been the value that's stayed with me throughout my journey to integrate my identities: black, woman, lesbian, nerd, feminist—among other things. I don't get it right sometimes. On some days, I still feel like puzzle pieces. Fragmented. And there are moments when I *do* choose, when some identities are more present than others. But not to the point of denial. I'm not sure highlighting one identity over another in any given moment is a bad thing; I have learned that it can, at times, be a survival tactic. Sometimes, when I'm sitting in the beauty shop—my all-black beauty salon, where there is a lot of Christian talk and no shortage of scripture-quoting—someone brings up the gay thing. I think to myself, "What is this going to turn into? Will I need to say something? Will I need to come out to these people? Should I?" Usually, the conversation ends up being pretty innocuous, but it is one of those moments when I question the safety of challenging homophobia in a place where I am in community with other black (and presumably straight) women. Should I be a black woman right now, or the black lesbian?

These days, I work in a campus women's center, and I present workshops and facilitate discussions about feminism to students who are the same age I was when I started this process. The f-word is still taboo and dirty and shunned like it's the plague—not always for the same reasons I shied away from it, but sometimes for *exactly* the same reasons.

I don't shove it down their allegedly postfeminist throats, because I remember what it was like to be insecure and thinking that feminism was static. Sometimes I dress it up in the terms that students seem to be more comfortable with: diversity, equity, social justice. A rose by any other name, right? My feminism isn't caught up in semantics 24/7.

But I do *own* my feminism. I have learned to challenge people who either directly or passive-aggressively try to convince me or dictate to me what movements belong to me. I do honestly tell folks what I think about the feminist Movement, capital M, the things I love about feminism, such as its incredible potential to include so many voices, and the things that frankly make me want to jump out of a window, like the rigidity and the exclusion that occurs when feminists don't realize that potential.

There are some moments when I'm so done with feminism. I'm over the WWIFAs, the White Well-Intentioned Feminists of America who do not want to own their privilege. I have those moments when I simply cannot support the notion that Girls Gone Wild represents a new brand of feminism and liberation. Holler back, feminism. I want no part of you. And then I'm back to being a womanist. Or a black feminist. Or just . . . me.

But then, I inevitably have an incredibly insightful discussion with my female friends, or I receive positive feedback from someone who received help or guidance about an issue from my office, and then I realize why I (sometimes) call myself a feminist. More important, I realize why I care about this work. I remind myself that, for me, feminism has always been about choice. It's about being able to choose what to call yourself, what to wear, what issues to take up, what battles to fight. What kind of feminist—or womanist, or person—would I be if I didn't at least respect someone's choice to locate themselves within feminism in a way that feels comfortable for them? Allowing everyone the space to experience their own unique "click" moment—that's the first step in creating that feeling of freedom and community, that same sense of belonging that I experienced in my own family and in my campus women's center over a decade ago.

⟳

FEMINISM, WARTS AND ALL

Marni Grossman

⟶

Sometimes it feels as though feminism was my consolation prize for surviving an eating disorder. I beat anorexia, and all I got was this battered copy of *The Feminine Mystique* and a complimentary Ani DiFranco CD. . . .

My mother likes to brag that she was the first girl in her high school to wear pants. She took my sister and me in strollers to pro-choice rallies. She told me I could be whatever I wanted to be, and I believed her.

But for a long time, my feminism lay dormant because there were other things to think about. Good grades, for instance. Or the complicated flowchart of alliances and long-held grudges that made up my circle of friends. There were calories to count. Food to avoid. Body mass index to calculate. Dulcolax or ex-lax? Razor blades bought in packs of ten and issues of *Vogue* magazine and Anne Sexton poems.

67

click

Anorexia changed everything, though. I tired of starving and bleeding and puking and crying. I wearied of living out my own personal reenactment of *The Bell Jar*. I got bored of my own bullshit. And then I became furious.

Social conscience is a funny thing. No one leaps out of the womb, arms raised, hands balled in fists, protesting injustice and decrying hypocrisy. And while I wish the facts were different, I delved headlong into feminism because I was sick of being hungry. I was sick of being silent and subdued. It hardly seemed fair. My girlfriends and I, we were all engaged in this elaborate, masochistic dance of self-loathing and self-denial. The boys, meanwhile, were speaking up. They were stepping up. They were seizing the scepter, grasping the keys to the kingdom, never once questioning whether or not they deserved it.

Why, then, weren't all the brilliant girls I knew kicking ass in science and making themselves heard? Like me, they were busy tallying up the entries in their food journals and straightening their hair. They were keeping their mouths shut because boys don't like girls who talk back. They were purging in the bathroom after lunch and slicing up their arms with the dull edge of car keys under their desks. *Reviving Ophelia* wasn't a cautionary tale for us. It was a how-to guide to being young, female, and fucked-up.

In the beginning there was this: I am ugly. My certainty on this point was absolute. Three little words that were imbued with such profundity, such truth. I felt it in my blood. My bones. My marrow. Mostly I felt it in the pit of my stomach, that hole that never seemed to get full.

My nose is long and angular. It meanders leftward. My hair grows dark and thick against white white skin. It grows in places it ought not to. Gravity compels my breasts to swing low, to droop. One is bigger than the other. I am asymmetrical.

I am an Egon Schiele painting. Vaguely indecent. Compelling. Hunched over from years of back-breaking worry.

The other girls at school didn't look like this. They were tall and tan and toned. They invited word choices like *lithe* and *lissome*. They didn't sweat. They didn't need to shave their legs or pluck their eyebrows or bleach their mustaches. Their breasts were perky and well-behaved. They were sleek and hairless and lovely. Everything I needed to be but couldn't. Or so they seemed to me.

If I can't be beautiful, I thought, *I will be thin. I'll be the thinnest, in fact. I'll be tiny and adorable and very, very good.*

Much has been written on the subject of starving. Reams and reams of gorgeous, heartbreaking prose by women more talented than I. Caroline Knapp, for example. Marya Hornbacher and Kathryn Harrison. They tell this story better than I ever could. And it's always the same story. It's always a variation on a played-out theme.

We think we discovered it. We think our tricks are unique. Feed the meal to the dog when no one is looking. Excuse yourself to the bathroom. Keep the water running to cover the sounds of half-digested pizza hitting water. Say you have a stomach flu. Tell them you're too nervous to eat today. Invent yourself an ulcer. But *Cosmo* already wrote that article. And we are not unique. We are legion. An army of the undead. An army of the sexless, the neutered. We are a lumpen mass of jutting limbs and squandered potential.

Life became a series of failures. Because when you are anorexic, you're always failing. You're always giving in to the temptation of a bag of M&Ms or a handful of popcorn at the movies. Even when you're asleep, you're guilty. You dream of lavish gourmet meals, and you wake up hungry. Hungry and desperately wanting.

69

click

You wanted so badly to be selfless. To be without need. You fail at this, too. Because though you'd never admit it, you want the most. You want to be a starving, pint-size martyr. You want someone to genuflect before your broken ninety-pound body.

I hoped that at my funeral someone would remark on how thin I looked. "You can see her ribs," they'd say admiringly. And in this way, I would win.

It sounds crazy. I know that. Death is not winning. Starving is not success. I know that and you know that. And yet.

I'm no anomaly. If this is madness, then it's a mass psychosis.

We fall for the mirage every time. We believe that thinness is next to godliness. We believe that less is always more. We believe that hunger is control and fullness chaos. We believe that cellulite is a moral failing and that washboard abs will bring about happiness and world peace. We believe this because they told us it was so. I didn't know this when I was sixteen. I know it now.

In her essay "Body Politic," Abra Fortune Chernik says, "gaining weight and getting my head out of the toilet bowl was the most political act I have ever committed." This quote has been cited hundreds of times. Every person who takes a women's studies class has read this essay. Professors put Chernik's piece on the syllabus because it rings true. It strikes a chord within every girl.

In insidious ways, we learned that our value is in our sex appeal, that our worth is our size-2 jeans. We were all raised to believe that, for women, thin and pretty are synonymous and if you're neither, you may as well not exist. Brains are irrelevant. Beauty reigns supreme. The patriarchy depends on our acceptance of this myth. It keeps us prone. Powerless before Cover-Girl and Trimspa and Lean Cuisine.

Putting down the laxatives and picking up Naomi Wolf was the most political act I have ever committed.

As I started to gain weight, I felt something inside me stir. Anger. Righteous indignation. The need to raise holy hell. And so I took to the library for answers.

My high school had a limited selection of feminist texts. In the months I spent recovering, I read them all. I read Nancy Friday and Susan Faludi and Elizabeth Wurtzel. I devoured Katha Pollitt and Betty Friedan, and I realized that my anger, selfish as it was, could—as theirs did—propel me into something wonderful. Feminism—warts and all—has a place. And while the media insists on forecasting the movement's imminent death, there are girls out there, desperate (as I was) to channel their anger into something more radical than self-hatred.

The Beauty Myth led to Susan Bordo. Susan Bordo led to bell hooks and Simone de Beauvoir. I wrote papers decrying the sexism in *The Taming of the Shrew* and *One Flew over the Cuckoo's Nest*. I created a heavy-handed art installation about the media's influence on female body image full of decoupaged magazine pictures and broken mirror shards. I went to college and became copresident of the Eating Disorder Reach-Out Service. I preached about the evils of the diet industry. I talked about air-brushing and read about fat activism.

But that was just the beginning. Organizing around issues of body image wasn't enough. Only the privileged, after all, starve themselves. What of women who didn't have that dubious luxury? What of trans women and sex workers and the girls toiling away in the maquiladoras? I declared a women's studies major. I went to work.

Some people receive a summons to do G-d's work. Me? I heard strains of Helen Reddy music. Feminism was calling.

There's an obvious flaw in this essay. It is disjointed. It's fragmentary. It does not flow. It's confusing and piecemeal and unpolished. There are too many incomplete sentences and too

click

many beginning with conjunctions or ending with prepositions. I agonized about this. I asked friends how to fix it. I put it aside for days and came back to it with fresh eyes. But no solution came to me.

I decided not to "fix" it. If this piece is disjointed and fragmentary and piecemeal, it's because that is how I came to feminism. There was no straight line. It was confusing and unpolished. I made mistakes. I will make more mistakes. But I won't apologize. I won't gloss over the nasty bits or cloak my anger in pretty prose. Feminism is not about perfection. It's about the power of speaking one's truth. Regardless of how ugly or raw that truth may be.

~⊚~

God, Sex, and Pythagoras

Shelby Knox

—

Geometry class, sophomore year, Coronado High School in Lubbock, Texas. I picked a seat in the back of the class, by the only other girl in the room, and introduced myself. "Can I just take the 'F' and not have to take the class?" My new seatmate smiled, introduced herself as Monica, pulled a fancy-looking calculator out of her bag, put it on the desk, punched in a series of numbers, and turned the screen toward me. Instead of numbers, green letters blinked, "Math SUX!"

Over the semester, we passed notes back and forth on the calculator, earning approving looks from the teacher for engaging in what she assumed were complicated machinations on the little machine. Monica and I both realized the social rules of our high school would prohibit us from being friends outside math class. She was a skater girl, one of the grungy kids whose friends dealt pot in the parking lot and mockingly crossed themselves when my group of churchgoing friends walked past.

click

In fact, she was one of the few people I talked to at school that
didn't go to my church. In our notes and short conversations
we carefully avoided topics on which we might disagree, including her tumultuous relationship with an eighteen-year-old
who'd graduated the year before.

The only relationship I was interested in that year was with
God. I sang in the choir on Sunday mornings, went to practice
to prepare for the annual mission trip on Sunday nights, and
taught children's choir on Wednesdays and then headed downstairs for youth group. Sophomore year was the first year we
could participate in "True Love Waits," a program developed
by the Southern Baptist Convention to help young people remain Biblically pure until marriage, and my friends and I were
excited to finally be old enough to talk about S-E-X.

I didn't admit it to my friends, but I had to look in the
dictionary to get a straight answer about what "sex" technically
meant. From what I could see on television, it involved lots of
writhing and screaming under the sheets for no apparent reason.
Whatever the mechanics, I already knew from a local youth pastor's presentation at school that it was dangerous for people my
age. His message was clear, and I remember his exact words: "Sex
within marriage is like fire in the fireplace—it keeps you warm
and makes you feel good. Sex outside of marriage is like fire in the
middle of the living room—it will burn your house down and ruin
your life. It can and probably will kill you."

During the ten-week course, we learned from the youth
pastor's wife that sex before marriage is a sin that marks you as
a "fallen woman" in the eyes of God and ruins you for any man
who might marry you. When the sessions culminated with a
pledge to remain a virgin until marriage, my father put a silver
band with the words TRUE LOVE WAITS on my ring finger and
I vowed, before God and the congregation, that I wouldn't be
one of those girls who ruined her life by being weak and stupid
about sex.

I also promised myself that I would talk to Monica about the dangers of sex and try to convince her to break up with her boyfriend. I knew she wouldn't like what I had to say, but I felt a responsibility to tell her what a horrible mistake she was making if she gave it up to that boy, which she'd intimated she might.

Monica wasn't in math class the next day, nor was she there for the entire week. When she did walk in the following Monday, she looked past me and our table and plunked down at a single desk on the other side of the room. I wondered how she'd known I planned to confront her. I tried to make her look at me by staring from across the room and instead noticed how tired and sad she looked. I started imagining what horrible thing could have happened to make her look so much older in just a couple of weeks. Part of me hoped that her boyfriend had broken up with her and we would both be saved (from an awkward conversation). After an agonizing fifty minutes, the bell rang and she raced out the door.

I caught up to her in the hall, put my hand on her shoulder to turn her around, and demanded, "What's the matter with you? Why didn't you sit by me?"

She looked at me with more anger and hurt than I'd ever seen in anyone's eyes and said, "You don't want to talk to me anymore. Leave me alone. I won't go to this school much longer anyway, so forget we ever met, and go away."

"Why in the world won't you go to this school? And I like talking to you. What's so terrible that we can't talk anymore?"

She studied me and then looked nervously around the hall, tears threatening to fall from her eyes. "Fuck, I'm going to regret this," she said with a choked laugh, pulling me by the hand into the bathroom.

"Just don't say anything to me, alright? I'm pregnant. Yup, I'm a slut and I'm going to hell and now you can go tell all your goody-goody friends about the big whore who didn't keep her legs shut." She glared at me, tears falling down her face. It was like she was daring me to say something.

I was shocked. I didn't know what to say or think. I blurted out, "How did you let that happen?"

That made her cry harder. "He said I couldn't get pregnant my first time," she explained. "He said he never used condoms because they don't work and nothing bad had ever happened before."

Slowly, she spilled the rest of her story. When she told her boyfriend about the baby, he'd called her a whore and swore up and down it wasn't his. He wasn't returning her calls, and she was terrified of what her father might do to her when he found out.

When I went home that night I was furious, but I couldn't pinpoint at whom or what. I couldn't stop hearing the hatred in Monica's voice as she called herself a whore and expected me to do the same. I considered being angry at myself for not talking to her about abstaining from sex earlier in the year, but that seemed so ridiculous now. She would have felt attacked and judged. She would have been right to feel that way.

The only way I could have helped her was to tell her she *could* get pregnant the first time and that condoms *do* work. All the judgment and fear and shame she'd learned in school and church had done nothing but make her despise herself after the fact. I was angry because she and I and all the other girls in our school deserved real information about how not to get pregnant. The adults we trusted had deliberately denied it in favor of abstract judgments and flat-out lies. I couldn't do anything to help Monica with her situation, but I could at least try to make sure it didn't happen to anyone else.

∽☙∾

THE RIGHT PITCH

Colleen Lutz Clemens

—

I became a feminist on the marching band field.

Though I never struggled with math and science (in fact, I did better on my math SAT than the verbal, a story I never fail to tell my students when bemoaning the emphasis on standardized tests in our No Child Left Behind world), I figured out pretty early in life that I needed to choose a humanities path. I joined chorus, though I really couldn't sing confidently, and took French, which I saw as a highway out of my working class family. Madame Koch, so sophisticated in her knotted scarf, showed me a world beyond Mack Trucks and The Steel, a world that didn't have harvesting times or government cheese. However, my first thrust into the arts came in fifth grade, when I began to learn how to play the clarinet.

My mom made me practice on the screened-in porch with the back door closed. Our neighbors in the row of townhomes heard "Mary Had a Little Lamb" squealing through their kitchen windows while they made dinner. My parents bought me the clarinet, not rented it, and this financial commitment sealed my fate with the black plastic, shiny-keyed "licorice stick." I bought Benny Goodman cassettes at the Woolworths. I rubbed cork grease on the instrument's joints. I invested in expensive reeds early in my playing; I watched what the girls who had private lessons did, and then I did the same. The clarinet section took up half the orchestral arc in the gym, but Timmy O'Donnell was the only boy. We stared at the flutists across the way; no boys sat among them.

Instead, the boys loomed over us from behind, always a bit higher on the stage. They held polished brass instruments and wooden mallets, which made loud, crashing sounds rarely in time with the conductor. When the delicate winds came in on patriotic songs and holiday arrangements, he would look back at them and passionately signal them to grow quiet, but *pianissimo* was not part of the boys' vernacular. There was no nuance in their performances; the girls barely noticed that our parents never heard us through the crashing of the boys.

Throughout middle school, I grew as a player, always playing first or second clarinet, starting to take on the headmistress role of entering the concert hall last, playing a high C as the rest of the band tuned to me. When the band members seemed content, I nodded and took my seat, where the audience watched the right side of my body for the rest of the evening. My *embouchure* improved. I sometimes practiced at home, but I belonged to several smaller groups, such that I played every day already. Wind ensemble. Orchestra. Pit band for plays. Jazz band when I took up tenor sax. Its heft made me feel strong. I relished putting the strap around my neck to hold the length of the sax. My hips and arms supported this new instrument as I held it at my side. But my delicate reed-worn lips and strong mouth muscles remained attuned to my clarinet as I left middle school.

Though not eager to join the marching band's clarinet line in high school—I was smart enough to understand the stigma attached to it—I realized I would be alone on Friday nights since all my friends would be marching at football games. To me it seemed a crude art, forcing Souza marches through my versatile instrument. What sounded melodic echoing through the auditorium's acoustics became shrill and screechy out in the open. The footwork became more important than the music. As we toe-heeled around the practice field remembering our stops, I missed the Mozart and Bach, whose performance never required sunscreen. New to the high school, I moved back down to the end of the first clarinets with the understanding I would find my way back to the top in a few years.

I listened to the section leader tune us, but by now all of the clarinetists were girls. Watching the football players' practice across the field became more important than finding the right pitch. Staring at them run, sweat dripping from under their helmets, made us feel the warmth of the day even more; they were the cute boys, the ones who would pair up with the popular cheerleaders practicing on the other side of the stadium, their silver pom-poms catching the August sun. In the end, though, the clarinetists and the cheerleaders shared a common goal: On the sidelines with our marches and their short skirts, we were to rouse the winning nature of the boys. Even so, we marched and marched all summer long. The woodwinds dated the brass or percussion line. They paired up, sometimes passing each other on the field as we made our way into an X formation.

The brass player I liked wasn't interested in a sophomore, so I watched from the lines as my friends found partners. Over bologna sandwiches and bug juice, I would talk to the other single members of the band. Mainly we talked about music, teachers, and cars and avoided the topic of dating. The tuba boys were all single, so we spent a lot of time together. They took great pride in the dented instruments they toted around the field in the heat. Their cheeks reddened at the great puffing required to emit a sound from the sousaphone. Our lunch chatter often turned to the virtues of the tuba and the glee of not having to wear the painfully dorky feathered band hat the rest of us wore; they donned red berets, slanted on the head to make way for the tuba that wrapped their bodies.

The day Ralph Ciotti said a girl couldn't play the tuba, a feminist angel got her wings. I sat on the grass astonished by his pronouncement, but in fact, his assumption felt correct. The girls held instruments of softness and light, just as they were supposed to walk in the world, while the boys banged with mallets and blew as hard as they could, making blaring cuts in the air with their brash sounds. His utterance of the unspoken gender rule in the band infuriated me. I needed to prove Ralph wrong.

Mr. Watson, our band director, loved music and would do anything to produce the best sound from our group. A composer who happened to teach high school, he wrote esoteric compositions that befuddled us, but his dedication to our excellence mesmerized us. Now a teacher myself, I laugh to imagine his response when a fine clarinetist approached him and asserted that in the next season of marching band she would play the tuba instead. He could have balked at my demand, but instead, he encouraged me and gave selflessly of his time. He confirmed that I would be the school's first female tuba player, and his joy at the thought fueled my drive to prove a girl could do it.

I didn't take into consideration that I was now going to have to relearn everything I ever knew about playing an instrument, even how to carry it. Now a junior in high school, I could hold my clarinet or saxophone case while juggling books and a Trapper Keeper, but the tuba required a full-body commitment from our first encounter. The instrument wound around itself like a snake waiting to be charmed out of the battered black case. I needed both arms to wrap around the circumference of the new beast. My lessons served as the training required to heft the instrument on a playing field, something I had not attempted yet. In his free time during the summer, Mr. Watson showed me how to assemble the bell to the body, the mouthpiece to the rest. No finesse required, no cork grease or shimmying: Simply insert the dulled metals into each other.

For the first two weeks, my parents banished me to the basement with this brute. My first attempts to push air through the body of the tuba resulted in the sound of spittle echoing through several feet of brass. My delicate lip muscles now had to learn how to purse, to make duck call sounds instead of placing my mouth around a smooth point. No reed was there to create vibrations; now the vibrations had to come from me. The most I could muster was a few farting sounds when I abandoned all decorum and blasted into the instrument.

At school, I left the rows of clarinets, nestled safely near the conductor, and headed to the back of the room, where the boys joked in between songs. Band gossip had spread the word that I was coming, but the boys still raised their eyebrows and poked each other in the ribs. I was terrible at the tuba, blurting out-of-tune notes, but no one seemed to mind or notice, even though my mistakes overtook the band. Being in the back row with the boys meant I couldn't hear what the rest of the band on the lower tiers was doing; I was free to make mistakes without understanding their ramifications on the rest of the group. I began to drown out the woodwinds, where I felt I belonged.

After a few weeks, the time to head out on the marching field arrived. I would now have to slip my body into the hole of the instrument and rest it on my shoulder for hours in the hot sun. The first day of carrying this strange creature left me missing the delicateness of my clarinet and wondering why I felt the need to prove a girl could play such an instrument; my doubt grew, but Mr. Watson's pride and the thrill of doing something I thought a girl shouldn't be doing propelled me

click

onto the field. The other tuba players were kind and patient with me, perhaps wondering how long I would actually last before quitting, though I did survive the entire season. My arm muscles grew ropey, my thin legs showed defined quads as day after day I learned that, in fact, a girl could play the tuba in the marching band, even if she didn't do it all that well. Once the season ended, I hung up my beret and didn't return to the marching field my senior year.

Every day that summer we worked on a Frank Sinatra number that was also the theme song to a popular show I detested: *Married with Children*. In it, the women played dim-witted sex-pots in leopard-print skirts, always bickering with the gross men in their lives. I hated the popularity of the Bundy family and didn't understand why the band was endorsing such a silly show based on machismo and misogyny. At the end of the song, the tuba line found its way to the center of the field for a solo; the last two notes of "Love and Marriage" were a descending blurt I came to regard as a noisy vehicle to express my disdain for the show, for a world where women should be tramps who circled around the men who made their lives miserable. I stood in the middle of the action, took a deep breath, and sent all of my budding anger through the tuba's body until it spoke for me in a voice louder than I had yet to know was inside me.

Born-Again Feminist

Jillian Mackenzie

———

My first bout of "women's lib" (as it was known in my 1970s childhood) struck early. But not so much as a moral calling. My fervor for gender equality took hold because it appealed to my contrarian personality—and because it was an ironclad weapon in a battle with my older sister, though not because she had traditional gender views. To explain, Alison was born during a short stint my British parents spent in Scotland for my father's medical training; I was born after the three of them had settled in Pennsylvania. And like most older sisters, Alison taunted me as a hobby. When she was age eleven to my age six, her preferred tack was the fact that she was Scottish and I was not. She acquired stuffed-animal Scottie dogs, a tam-o'-shanter coin purse, and a tartan comforter cover, explaining pityingly to me that only Scottish people could appreciate them. As the only person in the family born in the United States, I found it infuriating when she would pretend to marvel at some perfectly

83

click

mundane behavior of mine, like eating cake with a fork instead
of my hands (something, true, our British relatives didn't do):
"Oh, of course, you're *American.*"

Around the time Alison's Scottish nationalism was rivaling
Sean Connery's, I learned a crucial fact in school: Only people
born in the United States could become president. In that
moment, the game changed. I had a goal that I announced to
everyone, starting with my sister: I wanted to be the first female
president of the United States. (And she couldn't be.)

From there, I officially became a feminist—partly because
I was too stubborn to suddenly let any notion that went along
with my future presidency drop, and partly because, once I
started thinking about it, the idea that boys might have advan-
tages I didn't ticked me off. I was the smartest, and bossiest,
person in my small class, and there was no way a boy deserved
better grades, to cut the line for the tire swing, make the rules
in kickball, or eventually make more money than I would. And
even though I was really just out for myself, feminism was a
handy cover story. I was supported in fourth grade by the best
teacher of my life, also a women's libber. (Really, that's what
people called themselves then.) She encouraged me to formally
debate the class chauvinist in front of the rest of the fourth-
graders. Note cards in hand, we argued about why women
should earn equal wages and why a woman who worked wasn't
stealing a man's job—things that, in 1982, were still arguable.
I definitely won. At least as I recall.

But that was my youthful feminism's high point: Those
beliefs vanished during adolescence. I got pudgy, glasses, and
braces all at once, and my self-esteem collapsed. My bossiness
petered out with it. At fourteen, I went to a girls' boarding
school with very progressive, even feminist, beliefs (the headmistress had been a classmate of Hillary Clinton's at Wellesley)
and mostly Southern students. I loved those four years, but
instead of rekindling my feminism, high school stamped out the

last sparks. I was dying for a boyfriend and wasn't finding one, and feminism just seemed like an additional obstacle. Plus, the idea of having a guy pay and open doors for me seemed incredibly dreamy and romantic. I also developed an intense fear of public speaking—there went the presidential ambitions (not to mention, further debates).

Almost ten years of antifeminist attitude later, I was born again, like George W. Bush in a Texas prayer group. And like him, I remember the moment clearly. In 1992, the summer after my sophomore year of college, I was living on Martha's Vineyard with my boyfriend and a collection of friends, a dream summer. One of my two jobs was in a bookstore, and the store's owners put Susan Faludi's *Backlash* front and center on the first floor, in front of my cash register. It had an unmissable cover, the title in approximately fifty-point crimson red letters. But I think it was the subtitle, *The Undeclared War Against American Women,* that made me buy it: Wait, there's a war against *me?* Those words got my dormant (but apparently, not dead) selfish-feminist hackles up again.

I read the statistic-filled, wrist-strainingly heavy hardback cover-to-cover, like a novel. I brought it to the beach on my days off and would burn through a chapter or three before bed. Faludi made it a page-turner, just like the Armistead Maupin books my bookstore bosses always recommended to vacationing customers.

Faludi spoke directly to people like me, who had absorbed the previous few years' barrage of articles on "women over 30 are more likely to be struck by lightning than marry!" and "career women are miserable and lonely!" as kind of unfortunate but, well, they're in the news, so they must be true. She recalculated statistics, pointed out when an article was based solely on anecdotes or even misinformation, reinterviewed magazine article authors and had them concede, "The evidence was rather narrow." I was beyond galvanized; I was furious at how we'd all been misled. The topics of Chapters 5 and 6, movies and television, spoke to me in particular (I was a college student, after all). Suddenly, it was so clear: How had I not considered that there was something sick and bizarre about the fact that people rooted for Glenn Close's character to die in *Fatal Attraction?* Or that scene where Holly Hunter sobs alone in *Broadcast News*—come to think of it, that was totally inexplicable. Wait, on *Cheers*, Sam Malone wasn't funny and Diane Chambers an uptight buzzkill—he was a blatant sexual harasser, she was smarter than him, and he was trying to cut her down to size.

By the time I got to the section on "New Right" advocates who told women to stay home and leave work to men—women who themselves *worked*—I was not only fuming but changed for good. My self-esteem never bounced back up to that grade school level, but a bit of moxie replaced it. I began to point things out, both micro and macro. Why, I would ponder out loud while at home with my mostly male housemates, were all of the cashiers at the Martha's Vineyard grocery store female (I was one of them) while my two male housemates got the more interesting jobs in the bakery and salad bar? Why, I would ask while we watched the Summer Olympics, did female gymnasts wear makeup and get judged on their appearance? A bunch of liberal-arts students, the guys were an open-minded group—they would yell "Back*lashin'!*" whenever I began a lecture, but I didn't get any arguments. I like to think I at least made *them* think.

Thanks to that one book (although others followed), feminism became something that wasn't just about the risk that I personally might not get everything I deserved (or, for that matter, as a way to get back at my sister). It gave me the revelatory feeling that the world was not how I'd seen it before. I saw everything—not just my own experiences—in a new light. And I wanted everyone else to as well. Although I began following news on big-picture, international feminist issues like FGM, my most intense focus—and where I thought I could make a difference—was day-to-day experience, how men and women treat and interact with each other.

Back at college, surrounded by fellow psych majors and women's study minors, there weren't an awful lot of minds to change; even my then-boyfriend took women's studies classes for his major. But entering the world of dating in New York City years later, suddenly, all of the issues I cared about deeply were front and center—and I was finally in a position to influence people's thinking. For a few years in the early 2000s, I was single for the first time since age eighteen and found a group of friends in approximately the same situation. We drank and dated our way through the city. All we talked about were guys; feminism never damp-ened my interest in men and having (an enlightened) one as a boyfriend. My friends were hardly anti-feminist, but they weren't as hell-bent as I was and jokingly called me a femi-nazi—because they knew whenever a dating topic came up, I couldn't pipe down. I was like a missionary, determined to convert.

The topic that was the most common even among these forward-thinking women: money. When a friend would be an-noyed if a guy didn't pay on a date, or half-jokingly wish after a hell day at work that she could just marry rich and retire, I wouldn't be able to resist speechifying on economic indepen-dence. *Valley of the Dolls* was my tract-slash-cautionary tale—I would retell the most sordid parts, reminding everyone just how recently women had had to depend on catching a man for survival, how it was a slap in the face to our mothers' and grandmothers' generations to depend on men for money, how it set the stage for a life where you were dependent forever and had no escape.

click

I think I made a dent . . . or at least presented a point of view that encouraged a couple of friends to date adorable, younger hipster boys. Another great battle emerged when *He's Just Not That into You* was published. Almost every intelligent woman I knew bought and swore by it. On principle, I never read it, but as I heard over, and over, and over, the first bit advises that a woman should never ask a man out. When a friend would talk about not pursuing a guy, I would lecture that women had as much right to enjoy the chase as men, that if a guy was interested one phone call or email wouldn't turn him off, and most of all, if a guy was such a wuss that being asked out would scare him, why would you want to date him anyway? I definitely managed to rouse up some action with that point of view. Admittedly, that could have been because it's what my friends wanted to do anyway.

I continued to try to inject my feminist point of view whenever possible, as we all gradually paired off and found our long-term mates. The doors close a bit when someone gets really involved, and happily, among those women, it seems like there's no need for speeches or mind-changing. So now I'm in search of my next feminism-spreading frontier. Purchasing a copy of *Free to Be. . . You and Me* for everyone's new children—male and female—might be a good start.

NOT MY MOTHER'S HOSE

Courtney E. Martin

———

I would like to tell you that what made me a feminist
was the moment when my father slipped a signed copy of *Outrageous Acts and Everyday Rebellions* by Gloria Steinem in my
bookshelf when I was just a little girl. I would like to tell you
that I became a feminist while watching documentary films in
my living room night after night; my mom cofounded a wom-
en's film festival—now the longest running in the world—in
the '80s. I would like to describe the incredible women's studies
course I took at Barnard College and say that it was there—
surrounded by a gargantuan reader on globalization, feminist
philosophy texts strewn around outraged, pierced twenty-year-
olds—that I experienced my resounding click.

All of these things would be a little bit true. Certainly having feminist parents and an education firmly situated within a
feminist context contributed to my identity. But what would be
more true is that fishnet stockings made me a feminist.

click

Let me explain.

By the time I hit seventeen years old, I was pretty sure that there was something to all of this feminist stuff that my mom had been jabbering on about for years. I certainly wasn't about to admit that to her, but I began creeping into my parents' bedroom and plucking select titles off their bookshelf. *The Company of Women* by Mary Gordon. *Rubyfruit Jungle* by Rita Mae Brown. *The Beauty Myth* by Naomi Wolf. I was looking for an answer to a very specific question: Why are all of my friends and I falling apart?

Sounds like a case for Mary Pipher; my mom's copy of *Reviving Ophelia,* published the year I turned twelve, *was* dog-eared and underlined to the hilt. But it was something more complex than all that. We weren't just falling apart in the good old-fashioned ways—eating disorders, cutting, sex, and drugs. We were also cracking under our own outlandish expectations. We were the smartest kids in the school, the editors of the newspaper, the valedictorians, the presidents of every club. It was as if, on the surface, all of my mom's feminist dreams had come true. Girls really did think they could do anything, myself included. But underneath it all was an abyss of insecurity, self-destruction, and crippling perfectionism.

Why? I wondered in journal entries, written in the hand-writing I imitated from Mary Margaret Nussbaum, the year-older and so talented editor in chief of the newspaper. *Why?* I discussed with my little crew of rebellious girlfriends as we drank sickeningly sweet St. Ide's Special Brew and waited for our boyfriends to emerge, smelly and defeated, from the football locker room. *Why?* I whispered to the glow-in-the-dark-star-covered ceiling in my childhood bedroom.

It makes me sad now to think about how much of my first feminist searching was born out of such desperation. I wish I had come to feminism celebratory or even outraged. Instead I came like so many . . . on my knees, confused, heartbroken.

Barnard College proved to be a place where just about everyone else was in the same state of confusion I was. We were all whip smart, quirky, and intense, but none of us wanted to call ourselves feminist. It's comical to think of it now. Here we were, dorms full of spitfire girls who had chosen an all-women's college, and we were still reluctant to don the label. We were the low-hanging fruit, and feminism just hadn't managed to pluck us.

That changed for me the day that Amy Richards and Jennifer Baumgardner showed up on the third floor of Barnard Hall to give a talk on their new book, *Manifesta: Young Women, Feminism, and the Future.* Amy was plucky and compact, smart without an ounce of pretension, a no-nonsense beauty. Jennifer was her opposite—long and sinewy, bright blond, and yes, wearing fishnet stockings. Someone leaned over into my ear and said, "The blond one is dating Amy Ray from the Indigo Girls." My eyes grew wide and my palms began to sweat.

Best of all, they seemed to absolutely adore one another. They were besties, taking over the world with this totally fresh feminist analysis. This wasn't the swishy skirt feminism that my mom had manifested at her once-a-month women's groups. This was contemporary, witty, brash, even a little sexy. This was who I wanted to be.

I took *Manifesta* with me when I left for my semester abroad in South Africa shortly thereafter and devoured it on planes, on trains, and in my ant-infested bedroom. Honestly, I can't remember much of what was in that book. What I do remember is feeling connected. I needed to feel like my generation had a place in this centuries-old movement that reflected our sensibilities, our challenges, and, silly as it may seem, our aesthetics.

To this day, I ask myself, why did it matter so much? Why did I care so much that my feminism look like me, talk like me, walk like me? Why did appearance have anything to do with it? It feels as if, even by acknowledging this, I'm siding with the enemy; responding to Amy and Jen's style rather than their theories is like catcalling my own feminist big sisters. But it's the truth. And for all of its seeming frivolity, I think it's an important one.

I've seen it manifest in other times, in other places—most obviously with my crew at Feministing.com. When Jessica Valenti walks onto a stage with her hip haircut and throws a couple of unself-conscious f-bombs (fuck and feminist) around, I can see the crowd of young women learn forward in their seats. When Samhita Mukhopadhyay talks about tech, race, or gender on a panel, her bangles clanging together, her attitude ballsy and unapologetic, young people—women and men alike—swoon and take notes. When Miriam Zoila Pérez talks about midwifery, queer politics, and activism while flashing that irresistible smile and sporting a vest or a button-up, you can practically watch the lightbulbs go on above wandering, wondering twenty-year-old heads.

I've experienced it myself. After speaking on college campuses, especially in the Midwest, Texas, and the South, I consistently get emails from young women confessing that they had no idea that young feminists even existed, much less "cool" ones like me. I find myself—otherwise notoriously uninterested in contemporary fashion and low maintenance when it comes to getting ready—actually thinking about what I wear to these events in a very deliberate way. Sometimes the irony astounds me: I don't dress up for business meetings, but I do dress up for eighteen-year-old girls who might be converted to feminism by my knee-high boots or my trendy dress.

It's not that what I'm saying isn't significant. I know the content of my talks, the subject matter of my books, blog posts, and columns are all critical. Just as Amy and Jennifer were making an argument in *Manifesta* that has shaped a whole generation of young women, I try every day to contribute substantive insights and pose challenging questions so feminism can be even more inclusive and incisive. But we simply can't pretend like the cover on the book isn't being judged.

It's understandable that it's a sticking point for feminists. So much of our work is about de-emphasizing appearance, especially traditionally defined notions or racist ideals of beauty. The last thing we want to do is privilege appearance over substance. But, we also have to be real about the ways in which people get brought into political movements. It's rarely because we read up on legislation or resolve to be more active citizens. It's more often because we find a crew of people who we really like and we identify them with a fresh feeling for politics. Or we fall in love with someone and can't stand to be away from them when they go to the meetings. Sometimes, it's because we think the leader of an organization has dope style.

Black power had its afros and raised fists. Antiwar movements of the '60s had their bell bottoms and their John Lennon glasses. Hip-hop has its bright sneakers and gangsta lean. Obama Nation has its Shepard Fairey poster. Movements, whether we like it or not, are visceral experiences. Feminism is no exception. If we want to attract more young women into the fold, especially given how vilified feminism is in the mainstream media, we can't pretend that aesthetics are irrelevant. I'm not saying that we have to conform to traditional beauty standards to convert the Forever 21–shopping masses. But I am saying that manifesting a personal style—hairy armpits or fishnets, gender queer or definitively feminine, hip-hop or hipster—doesn't hurt the cause.

Once we render the next generation defenseless with our vintage blazers and our fly Air Force 1, then we can capture them forever with our transnational feminist theory and intersectional analysis. Feminism transforms hearts and minds, but sometimes it has to be easy on the eyes first.

∽⊚∾

I Was Not Aborted and Further Miscellanea

Winter Miller

⸺

In August 1973, seven months after *Roe v. Wade* legalized abortion, some hippies (actually, my parents) discovered that the state of Massachusetts would not issue me a birth certificate. The reason was that my parents had given me my mother's last name, but the county registrar wasn't having that because, not only was my father's paternity established, they were married. I like to imagine that if we were included in Matthew 1:2 (proof the Bible begat the *Times'* Sunday Styles wedding section) the listing would have read: Cornelia Ann Miller and Albert Henry Norman begat Winter Norman Miller.

So the county registrar, a man of great moral principles, I have no doubt, rejected the birth certificate with Miller. When my parents protested, it was kicked back to the Massachusetts attorney general. Apparently no one in Massachusetts had encountered this circumstance, but after four months of researching English common law, the attorney general issued a decision. My parents heard from a reporter at *The Boston Globe:*

[*]MANLI HO: *How do you feel about your daughter getting your last name?*

MOM: *What?*

MANLI HO: *Oh, the attorney general ruled today that your daughter got your last name.*

MOM: *YIPPEEEEE! ALBERT, GUESS WHAT, SHE GOT IT!*

[*]Recollection *of actual conversation from my mother's memory. Names have not been changed to protect the innocent.*

My name set the precedent: From then on, in Massachusetts, even where the paternity of the father is established and where the child's parents are married to each other, a child may be given the mother's last name. Victory. Sweet. No doubt I drank a lot that night and shit my pants, just like every other night in those heady days of infancy. The community gave my parents a rough time, the newspaper printed a nasty editorial, and someone (*maybe the county registrar?*) sent a hate letter to Mr. and Mrs. Alberta Miller. My mom named the dog Mrs. Albert Norman since there wasn't one.

The poet and author Adrienne Rich has a great essay on Compulsory Heterosexuality—I put it in caps, because that's part of the title—and in it she lays out the evidence that because most of us are raised in a culture that views heterosexuality as normal, we innately label any other expression of sexuality as deviant. Even if we don't go around murdering the Matthew Shepards of the world—Matthew was beaten and tortured to death for being gay—it's latent, this idea that it's natural to be heterosexual.

I mention this because I think what we had in my house was kind of a Compulsory Feminism, which I put in caps here so you get the homage to Rich and in case someone wants to take that title and make a scholarly article with it.

So in fact, even during those first months when I didn't have a last name legally, I still had this intentionally gender-neutral first name. Compulsory Feminism from the get-go. I was about four when my mom and I had this conversation:

WINTER: *Mom?*

MOM: *Winter?*

WINTER: *How come you named me Winter?*

MOM: *We wanted a name that was not gender specific and was unusual. If someone saw your name on paper, they would have no idea what they were getting. It's androgynous.*

WINTER: *Oh. I'm going to call myself Harriet Begonia.*

MOM: *That sounds fine, Harriet.*

WINTER: *Call me Sherry the Dog.*

MOM: *Sherry the Dog it is.*

WINTER: *If I was a boy, would my name be Winter?*

MOM: *I knew you'd be a girl.*

WINTER: *How? The doctor told you?*

MOM: *Nope. I just knew. I also knew the date you would be born and that you would have a lot of black hair.*

WINTER: *Did I?*

MOM: *Yup.*

WINTER: *But if I had been a boy would I be named Winter?*

MOM: *Probably. No reason not to.*

I had the same conversation with my dad, only I had it at his house, because by the time I was two they had separated.

WINTER: *Why is Winter my name?*

DAD: *Your mom wanted it.*

WINTER: *But why?*

DAD: *If you were a boy we would have named you Vermont.*

It was a short conversation because my dad had a way of saying things where you didn't know if he was joking or not and you didn't want to appear gullible.

click

Oh, so the split, right—they divorced without a lawyer and agreed to share custody fifty-fifty. They were patting themselves on the back for their equitable ways. They thought they were so cool, acting so agreeable about the whole thing. Don't get me wrong, they were cool, but getting divorced didn't seem like a cool thing for at least the next fifteen years.

These were well-meaning people, my parents. So egalitarian with their shared custody they couldn't see that I hated going back and forth *and back and forth and back and forth* all the time. I lived three days with one parent, then swapped. Then we alternated week to week. Then we switched every two weeks. I appreciate *in theory* that they were sharing child-rearing, but it was disorienting to bounce back and forth. I wanted them to get back together, or at least live in side-by-side homes with a shared porch.[*]

[*]There was a double house like that on High Street, and I campaigned for us to all move in there.

They would say things to me individually, like:

DAD: You have two parents who love you so much, we both want to have you at our house. Some kids have parents who don't want them at all.

MOM: I think I'm a better parent to you than your father. You should live with me.

What they had in common when it came to me is that they each viewed me as sort of a walking, talking bumper sticker for their beliefs—throw a T-shirt on me, hand me a sign, and I'm anti-nuke, or pro-sisterhood, or I want Geraldine Ferraro for veep. When I was seven or so, my dad had this blue shirt with white letters: I'M PRO-CHOICE AND I ORGANIZE.

WINTER: What does pro-choice mean?

DAD: It means a woman can choose if she wants to have a baby or not, because it's her decision, not the government's.

My mom was a little more specific about things:

MOM: It means a woman who gets pregnant can decide if

she wants to give birth or have an abortion.

WINTER: What's abortion?

MOM: It's when you go to a doctor to end the pregnancy so you don't have the baby. It's important that it's legal so women can get them in hospitals. I had one.

WINTER: You did? What do you mean? (*As in, wait, was I aborted and came out anyway?*)

MOM: I was pregnant before you. You would have had an older brother.

WINTER: I want an older brother.

MOM: I wasn't ready before. I chose to have you, but after you I got my tubes tied. The doctor was an asshole; he wouldn't do it until I had your dad's permission because he was my husband.

WINTER: What tubes?

This was kind of the way these conversations went. It was never a simple answer. I do fault my mother for being a little too graphic with me and for not necessarily being developmentally appropriate. On the other hand, I did have a lot of information at my disposal.

The net result of the parents I had is that there was no *aha* moment when it came to being a feminist, a democrat (I toyed with socialism for at least a weekend)—these values were the ones humans were supposed to have. If you thought you should dress a girl in pink and a boy in blue you were obviously some kind of backwoods asshole. I thought my parents had the right values, like we were the good guys and if you disagreed with us, you needed to be schooled.

I've answered questions about my name for so many years now, I take the shortcut when I can and say they were hippies. But it's not that they were hippies; it's really that they were feminists. There's a picture of me from my third birthday: I'm wearing a fake gold watch and a white tank top with the women's symbol and a fist—the sisterhood is powerful logo. That's just the way it was.

click

My mom gave me these folktales for kids, *Tatterhood* and *Maid of the North*. The heroes were girls. I remember being six years old and going to an anti-rape march with my mom. It was dark and there were all these women holding signs and chanting. It was exciting (*past bedtime!*), but I was concerned (*all men raped?*). Also, I just couldn't make sense of the placard *Take Back the Night*. What could that possibly mean? No offense to the creators of that slogan, but it's kind of a misnomer, as if people only get raped at night.

So bully for me, right? I had these feminist parents who gave me a gender-neutral name and forced me to stick up for myself as soon as I could talk. It worked. Recently I was playing coed soccer with my colleagues, and some guys were great at passing the ball to women, some could have used some work. It's often the language that riles me:

MAN: Oh man, that guy was such a pussy, I didn't come near him.

WINTER: Let me ask you something? How do you feel about pussy, you like it or you don't like it?

MAN: I love it.

WINTER: I understand. So unless you love that guy, love what he did, it doesn't make sense to call him a pussy, since you love pussy.

MAN: It doesn't mean that. It's like, his shit is weak.

WINTER: I look weak to you?

MAN: No, but it's not literal, it's just a figure of speech.

WINTER: How about this, call him a cock next time. When you find something you dig, be like, that's so pussy!

But back from the political to the singularly personal, there was one thing that threw my feminist parents for a loop. Well, actually, just my dad. See, I broke up with my high school boyfriend, the captain of the football team, when I got to college, and at orientation[*] the biggest dyke on campus asked me out. [*]insert joke here.

DAD: "I agree with Freud on this, everybody's bisexual. I just don't want to see you get hurt; being gay is a hard road."

WINTER: Then why don't you see what you can do to make that road a little easier? You can start by accepting me and offering your support.

He asked me not to tell anyone else in the family that I dated women—not my younger sisters, not my grandmother, to whom I was particularly close. It was awkward, painful, and frankly, from Mr. Liberal Activist, a big letdown. I wanted to bring my dad to the town's gay parade, but he wouldn't march with me. He and I marched at a pro-choice rally that January, commemorating *Roe v. Wade*. He was as proud of me as I was of him for marching in front of the Boston State House together. "My body, my choice." But for my dad that May, pro-choice didn't include homosexuality.

There's something especially disappointing when you think your parents are the greatest, the coolest—they're your role models for how you want to live in the world—and you find out, in this intimate circumstance, hey, this father of mine, who has shown himself to be pretty evolved for a white dude, has a massive flaw in his identity politics. So he could say, "everyone's bisexual," but what he meant was closer to: I'm invested in your heterosexuality, and I'm not going to lift a finger to make it easier for you in the world, even though I'm an activist. He's grown up a lot in the last seventeen years. In his professional life, as a lobbyist for senior citizens, he has testified eloquently about the fundamental rights of gay couples to have the same marital privileges as couples who can marry. Massachusetts is a place where gays can legally wed. I believe my father was a part of changing that outdated prohibition as well.

My mom was a different story.

WINTER: I wanted to let you know I'm dating a woman.

MOM: I'm so proud of you! That's wonderful! What's she like? Can I meet her? I always wanted to be a lesbian, women are so great! I tried, it just wasn't for me. I'm so happy for you! How brave!

She's feminist to the core. She believes in equal rights for everyone. She dislikes patriarchy, and she's ignored it every step of the way, and the woman has never wavered. It's like this piece of me is descended from Annie in *Annie Get Your Gun* and I'm saying anything you can do, I can do, too. Not better, but just as well. Better than some, worse than others but not based on qualities rooted in gender or sex.

Despite my feminist DNA, there are still times when I catch myself behaving in a way that is rooted in our inherently pro-heterosexual—and also sexist—values. For instance, whom do I find attractive and why? There are complicated factors at work here, but it's worth pointing out that aside from my first girlfriend—the militant dyke (who incidentally dropped me on my ass after just a month)—nearly every woman I've dated has either never been with a woman before me or can just as easily pass as straight. It's hard to know where the lines blur, between internalized homophobia, compulsory heterosexuality, the laws of attraction, and good fashion sense.

When I first started dating women I was pleasantly surprised that women I found to be sexy and smart and fun wanted to date me. I felt a one-upmanship, as it were, as if I were flicking the bird at the boys who were the types to get the girl, and I was saying, *ha, brother, I stole your girl out from under you.* I have, in fact, stolen several very beautiful, smart women out from under the noses of their beautiful, smart boyfriends. I have never—to my knowledge—taken a girl who belonged to another girl. I guess that's my interpretation of the Code of the Samurai.

I have retired from recruiting (accidentally, on purpose) straight girls into the fold. Truth be told, I think we all exist on a continuum of sexuality that is as fluid as our society is tolerant. Labels mean little to me, personally, although I think *feminist* is a good one, as our culture evolves. But it makes sense to choose a partner comfortable choosing me. I'm looking forward to something conventional, like mating for life, raising a family. I owe a lot to my trailblazing parents for setting my default position to feminist. I expect my great-grandchildren will be equalists.

THE WOMEN'S CENTER

Olessa Pindak

———

My mother wanted boys. She was a teacher, and in her mind, girls were prissy, gossipy, giggly, and mean. Boys were fun, playful, strong, and solved problems with a punch. In 1976, she had one daughter and in 1979, another (me). She and my father decided simply to raise us as fun, playful, and strong individuals—feminists from day one. Our doctor, dentist, and vet were all women so that we would never understand that wasn't the norm. My mom mowed the lawn, pulled the weeds, and painted the house. My father taught us about his toy trains and how to fix his pinball machines. His bedtime stories were about semiconductors, and he bought us toolboxes for our birthdays. I grew up hating puffy sleeves, ruffles, and anything itchy. I fell off my bike and down a flight of stairs. I got scraped knees, ticks, and stitches in my chin and on my ankle. Barbies were banned from the house, as was most television and Saturday morning cartoons.

click

Our brand of feminism came directly from the school of Anna Quindlen. She began writing her op-ed column in *The New York Times* in 1981, and my sister and I grew up listening to my mother read it out loud to us over breakfast. Anna taught us about the difficulties we would face in our lives as American women and what it meant to be a modern feminist—how to be angry and to keep a sense of humor. Early on, my mother taught us what she called the "Paddington stare." It was a long, unwavering look of fixed anger and contempt and was reserved especially for men that made any sort of sexist remark. She would employ it during dinner parties, at the bank, or at the grocery store, and it silenced them immediately. I used to practice it in the mirror.

My mom and I went to see Anna Quindlen speak when I was a junior in high school. She talked about feminism and said it was time for the feminist movement to include men. She said without men becoming feminists as well, the movement would not march forward. She introduced the notion of humanism, and my mom quickly jumped on board. I wasn't sure how I felt about it. Now all of a sudden, we were supposed to be human-ists? What about all those years of rallying around women? Now we had to include the boys?

I went off to college a year later, and it turned out that it was a good time to be thinking about bringing the boys along because suddenly I was encountering them everywhere. For the first time in my life, there were boys in a girls-only bathroom, with a sheepish half grin. They were in our beds on Saturday evenings and Sunday mornings, and as I drifted off to sleep at night during the week, I could hear their shouts outside the window or loud laughter down the hall. They all missed people back home and had pictures and memorabilia around their rooms. They wanted to talk—about where we were drinking that night, the girls they liked, classes, their sports, the food in the cafeteria. It was easier than it ever had been in high school to be friends with them. Were these the boys Anna was talking about? Surely I could bring them along.

One of the first classes I took at college was Women's Studies 101. We read Charlotte Perkins Gilman, Virginia Woolf, and Margaret Sanger, and my passions about feminism were confirmed and ignited. We learned about women trapped by circumstances, and the idea of being sent away for bed rest and circling a room like in "The Yellow Wallpaper" made me furious. How lucky I was not to live then. We learned more about the struggles of women internationally, and the images of women in the Middle East who had to wear burkas and were being beaten for things like painting their nails haunted me. I cut out photographs of them from a magazine and hung them on my wall to remind myself to appreciate my freedom and stay angry.

One of our first assignments in that class was a group project, and my group met in the room of one of the few male upperclassmen. As we worked, his seven roommates stopped in during our meeting, eager to talk, to impress us, and ultimately, to mock the things we were studying. Growing up without brothers, the sheer maleness of all of these smart, funny boys in one place astounded me, and I found myself giving in to their taunts about angry feminists and laughed along with them about the material. Who needed feminism in the modern world? they questioned. Only really angry girls, they answered each other. The implication was clear: Those angry girls were not ones that they would want to hang out with. I questioned and bantered, but ultimately, I gave in. I left their room angry at myself, but just as excited as annoyed.

Through my coursework, I also became involved with the women's center on campus, a room that was lined with books about feminism and human rights, where student groups would meet to discuss the misogynistic culture of the fraternities and general objectification of women on campus. I would go to screenings of movies, like *If These Walls Could Talk,* in three parts, with discussion groups after each one. I loved the women I met there—smart, strong, unique. None of them were giving in to the culture on campus. They were there, supporting each other, trying to make waves, and I was torn. My politics were so aligned with these women, but as we worked on fliers that depicted Marilyn Monroe's womanly curves to raise consciousness about standards of beauty, my ears would perk at the sound of screams and deep male laughter on the walkway beneath us. I would leave the meetings and dash back to the dorms, where I would meet up with my other friends and go to the bars and fraternity parties.

I tried to bring the women's center out into the campus. I would get into heated political discussions late at night in the basements of frat houses. I would sometimes leave the room when my male friends started talking about women in a degrading way. But I would also hang out in dorm rooms with friends who kept pornography on their TV ten hours a day. More often than not, I gave in. I started to feel like it was impossible to fight the system, to be angry at every misogynistic comment that was made. I knew women that did it—that would never be friends with the men or women that I had befriended, but I chose instead to pick my battles. What was the difference, I thought—would I ever really change them anyway?

I joined a sorority, pledging sisterhood and feeling dishonest about the sisterhood of feminism that I had silently but seriously vowed to back in high school. I exercised a free love brand of feminism and took boys home to smooch all night. I dated a series of men who were wrong for me—one who lectured me on the differences between men and women (men are decisive; women can't make a decision), another who told me he would never marry a woman who wouldn't change her name. I began to wonder if it even mattered—maybe all men felt this way. Stuffed into my journals filled with entries about friends, men, and dating were GORE LIEBERMAN 2000 and

VOTE PROCHOICE bumper stickers. In between musing on love and crushes was musing about feminism and what it means and how it was shifting. I always seemed to come back to the question, "Are we really equal?"

I took a class called Masculinity. It explored what it meant to be a man in our culture, and it was the first time I had thought that it was hard to be a man, too—that any time a society had prescribed roles for its people, it was unfair. The reason I identified so strongly as a feminist is because I didn't want women to have to fit into a box—I wanted them to be unique, loud, unpredictable, strong, smart, and large. I wanted them to behave like men—to own their sense of self, do great things, and be confident. But did men feel the same way? Were they wishing they could nurture children, run a household, have more of a say in reproduction? Were there things that we had that they didn't?

I stayed friends with those men I met in my first women's studies class. We saw each other at parties, hung out in their dorm room, laughing, debating, arguing. They loved to talk to me about women's rights and took great pleasure in goading me on, watching my anger rise and my temper flare. I took another class with some of them—this one called Prostitution & Pornography. We debated the legalization of prostitution, and they laughed at Justice Stewart's "I know it when I see it" comment about obscenity.

During their senior year they played a prank and stole the women's center sign, ripped off the "w" and the "o," and hung it triumphantly in their dorm room. I wish I could say that I took a stand, that I called campus security and turned them in. That I made the statement that I had been leading up to in all those shouting matches. I didn't. And my fury and a door slam did nothing to tamp down their jovial and buoyant exuberance over their great win. It made me furious, but I also saw that they were honest in their convictions—they honestly didn't see any need for a women's center, and if I was going to be preaching equality, then the men should certainly have a center of their own as well. In their eyes women were equal—what was the fuss about?

I realized then that the difference between us was that I saw what the fuss was about. As I looked around the campus I had called home for four years, I saw date rape drugs, misogynistic comments flying around dorms, and fraternities that were known for their aggressive attitude toward women. I saw it in the larger world that I was about to enter, too—that as long as women were out of kitchens and in boardrooms, it didn't matter to most people that they weren't 50 percent of Congress, or even close. That the number of female CEOs or the pay gap wasn't registering. That as long as women could technically do anything they wanted, the barriers to allowing that to happen didn't seem to matter. Slowly, I got my conviction back. Those years of feeling like maybe I was wrong, perhaps my viewpoint had been skewed, were incorrect. I was on track. I realized I would never win a fight with those boys, but that the discussion was still important.

College is, in so many ways, about trying on different things and seeing what fits. It was no different with feminism. I had to wear the title into the world and see how it held up when things came into the room to intercept it. In those years, it became awkward, like when you get breasts and have to walk through the cafeteria, you have to learn to own them. And gradually, I did. I learned how to love being a feminist despite the difficulties. I learned that in the face of challenge, you either change your mind and decide it's not worth it, or you sit down and decide not to budge. For me, feminism didn't come with a bang, but a sustained whisper. Like all monikers, feminism has defined me, given me direction, and shaped my opinions and values. It didn't stop being relevant, and in the end, I didn't give up on it.

Feminism grows, matures, and means different things at various stages of life. My dentist is now a man. My boss is a woman. My boyfriend is a feminist. There were two major female candidates in a big election year. Things are changing. But they are frustratingly slow. I am still friends with those boys-turned-men who stole the women's center sign. Many are married, and they've partnered with strong, interesting women. They sit on boards of women's rights organizations; they're starting families and spending a lot of time around young people that they encourage to be strong—regardless of gender. We still gather together and sit around tables or living rooms and debate. They've come closer to my side—and I've learned how to debate more constructively.

I wonder sometimes about that sign they stole. I visited campus a few years ago and was happy to see that a new sign was up. The men's center one is long gone, thrown out at the end of the year, and buried when that joke was done. But the women's center sign was replaced and was once again flapping against the brick student center, comforting women, pressing buttons, furthering the discussion, proudly present, and brighter than ever.

～◎～

I Was a Secret Rich Kid: A Tale of Class Unconsciousness

Karen Pittelman

⟋

I was up to my arms in a sink full of greasy hamburger trays in southern New Mexico when it hit me. Bernice and I were doing the closing dishes. "How did you end up here?" she asked. I told her my boyfriend and I had been traveling from place to place, taking odd jobs for a month or two, then moving on. "Oh, I know how that is," she said sympathetically. I'd already been working with her at McDonald's for a few weeks, long enough to understand what she meant: *I know how that is when you have to keep moving, looking for some place cheaper, trying to stay ahead of your debt.*

I stared down at the soap and my rubber gloves, stunned. Was that what I wanted her to think? Was that why I had come here? Did I imagine I could just pack up, trek west, and magically turn into someone else? The truth was that I was moving around because I chose to. I'd graduated in the spring from an Ivy League university, and with a year before my partner and I had to go to Boston so he could start grad school, I'd wanted to drive cross-country.

At least that was the story I told myself. Road trips hold a special appeal for people with something to hide, and I was definitely in the midst of a cover-up. At the end of my senior year, I'd found out that I had a $3 million trust fund. I'd always known my family was wealthy. I grew up on the Upper East Side in New York City, went to an elite private school. Yet we never actually talked about money—and I was ordered to never, ever discuss it with anyone else.

Somehow I'd made it through most of college before I really understood *I* was rich, not just my family. Finding out about the trust fund was a wake-up call I didn't want. *Brrrng brrrng* went a diamond-studded phone with Richie Rich on the line. *Hey rich girl, who do you think you are?*

It was a good question. I wasn't much of a radical when I first got to school, but I'd left hoping to follow in the footsteps of the feminist, activist poets I admired like Adrienne Rich and Audre Lorde. Or June Jordan, who said, "You cannot write lies and write good poetry." Still, no matter how desperately I wanted to write good poetry, I had no clue how to tell the truth about my life. The problem with telling the truth is that then you have to do something about it. I could analyze and deconstruct it all in the abstract, but I'd never heard anyone talk about being rich and committed to social justice at the same time. It seemed like an impossible contradiction.

I did have a sense that there were things I needed to unlearn. I'd volunteered for a summer at a daycare center that served homeless families and seen how the four-year-olds I chased around the playground had already been forced to live through more in their short lives than I had. I started to wonder why the safety net I'd grown up with was meant only for me. The story went that we deserved our wealth, that it was due to hard work, intelligence, ingenuity. We never talked about luck. No one mentioned words like *race* or *gender*. The fact that there were people all around us who were just as smart and worked just as hard, whose three jobs barely covered expenses and provided no benefits, never figured into it at all.

Slowly, I began to realize that my own experience tore right through this logic of entitlement. I didn't have to work very hard. In fact, I could be stupid and utterly lazy, and I would still be rich. Could I really go along with this belief that wealth was merit based, that the rich deserved to be rich? Was I willing to live with its unspoken corollary: that the poor deserved to be poor?

I was overwhelmed. I didn't know how to untangle myself from what I'd been taught. I said I believed in a more just distribution of wealth, and yet I had a $3 million trust fund in my name. Suddenly, hitting the road became irresistible. I ignored the fact that it was this same privilege, no matter how cheaply I lived while I was traveling, that allowed me to make the decision to go in the first place. With no college loans to pay back and no family obligations, I was free in a way most people weren't.

I hadn't planned to run away or pretend to be someone else. As I stared silently at those dishes, though, I knew that was exactly what I had done. I don't think I said much to Bernice that day. Maybe mumbled something about a cross-country trip. But in that moment, I realized my past wasn't going anywhere. And neither was my privilege. No matter where I went, they were both coming with me.

I didn't have any illusions that my $3 million could change the world. Though I knew it certainly had the power to make a difference in a few people's lives. For me, the question became one of complicity. Should I take a stand? Or go along with the way things were, be the girl that I was raised to be? I didn't want to turn my back on my beliefs, and I didn't want to lie anymore about who I was. As the months and miles passed, my resolve grew. By the time we got to Boston, I had decided to empty my trust and give the money away.

On the one hand, being a class traitor was great. It turned out that plenty of people were talking about how to use class privilege for social change—I just hadn't met them yet. There were people all over dedicated to social justice philanthropy, who believed in activist-led giving and a more democratic grant process. There was also a whole generation of rich kids who had come before me, who'd felt the same way, taken action, and gone public about it. I even found a new group of young people with wealth, called Resource Generation, who were meeting to challenge each other to support social change.

For the first time in my life, I felt like my actions and my beliefs were finally lining up instead of contradicting each other. I had taken all the money out of my trust and turned it into a foundation. Then I'd started working with some amazing activists to turn it into a fund that was run by and for low-income women in Boston. I couldn't wait until the new board and director were ready to start and I could transition out, transferring the decision-making power to them.

On the other hand, being a class traitor sucked. Battling my family for control of my trust had made us all miserable. There hadn't been any other way to do it; with no legal authority over the assets, I'd had to fight for their permission to dissolve it. It took a year until my family agreed, on the condition that I create a foundation of my own instead of just giving the money away. Meanwhile, most of the people I grew up with thought I was nuts. I wasn't surprised—what did I expect? A parade?—but it still stung. At least this was all behind me, I thought. Maybe it was where I came from, but it wasn't where I was going. I was done with that world, done with being called Commie Karen, crazy and naive.

That's why, as I was sitting on the grotty floor of a church in Philadelphia, a woman from the Kensington Welfare Rights Union (KWRU) was about to say the last thing on earth I wanted to hear. It was the summer of 2000, the protests at the Republican National Convention were in full swing, and I was feeling rather pleased with myself. Nonviolence training? Check. Nonhierarchically organized band of fellow radicals? Check. Backpack with vinegar and bandannas in case of tear gas? Snacks in case we got hungry? Check. I felt like I was finally coming into my own as an activist, that I knew where I was and why.

The woman at the front of the room was talking about one of KWRU's founding principles: The movement to end poverty must be led by those who are under economic fire. Then she looked at us. "This doesn't mean there isn't work for you to do, too," she said, "even if you're not poor. Yes, you can come march with us, support us, follow our leadership. But you also have to go back. We all have to organize where we're from."

I wanted to scream. *No! Anything but that!* Then I started to question why I was so horrified at this idea and so thrilled with my new status as traitor. Maybe I hadn't come as far as I'd thought from that moment in New Mexico, washing dishes with Bernice. In a way, I was still hiding. I imagined that I could divest, set up this foundation, and be finished. But the privilege was still part of me. It ran much deeper than that money (though even giving it all away was an illusion—my family was still rich and willing to support me whenever I needed help). It was about access and connections. It was in my body itself, from the way I knew how to shake someone's hand to my straight teeth. I understood how that privileged world worked the way only an insider could. Who else was going to organize there? Who else would they even let in the door? If I was always going to have this power, I needed to find a way to use it for what I believed in. There was no such thing as done.

I've spent the last nine years since then trying to understand what it means to organize where I come from. It led me to work and write for Resource Generation, to join their mission to organize young people with wealth to support social justice. It took me to philanthropy conferences, where I tried to help promote more democratic, transparent ways of giving. It pushed me to step forward and talk publicly about my decisions in hopes of reaching out to other rich kids who might feel the same way. At first I wanted to jump up and down with a megaphone and screech at them to join us. I had to learn how to meet people where they were. How to listen. How to struggle together to break down the ways we'd been taught to keep our privilege entrenched.

This work feels increasingly vital to me because, while there are plenty of wealthy people on the left, many of them in hiding, we rarely talk about how class privilege affects and undermines our movements. We talk about funding—how to get it, how to hold on to it—but we don't name the dynamics that arise when activists who keep their class privilege undercover act out. It may be by always taking charge, or by demonstrating a lack of sensitivity to others' financial obstacles, or by using connections to fundraise without ever sharing them. We undermine our ability to work collectively if we can't even name these patterns, much less address them when they surface. And when we coddle donors, allowing them to determine the direction of organizations and movements by what they're willing to fund, the price is a steep one.

I believe it's the role of people with wealth to call out these dynamics, to inspire each other to take action, to give away as much money as possible, to question when we should take leadership and strive to step back, to challenge the very institutions that gave us our power and privilege in the first place.

The master's tools may never dismantle the master's house, but they ought to be good for something. We can at least use them to take a big chunk out of the drywall on the way to tearing the place down. The myth of the level playing field is a core justification for the unequal distribution of wealth. Rich people, especially inheritors, need to come forward and tell the truth about just how unlevel this field is. It's our job, as those who have seen the inner workings of how wealth is created and privilege is reproduced, to help shatter that myth.

Of course I understand why people with class privilege would rather keep it hidden. I don't want to forget all the ways I'd hoped to hide my own. Yet when we bury our stories, we abandon one of our greatest political strengths. What I love about feminism is the idea that telling the truth about our lives is a radical, transformative act. Still, it can be easy to fall into the trap of thinking some truths are nobler than others, to romanticize what it means to be oppressed and to conceal what it means to have power.

But we will never understand how the whole system works until we can tell both sides of the tale. The story of the woman paid less than a living wage is tied to the story of the woman whose family owns the chain of stores that benefits from her labor. Bernice's story—how she got to that sink at McDonald's with me, trying to make ends meet—is irrevocably tied to my own and the ways that a handful of families like mine have been permitted to build their wealth at everyone else's expense. It's easy to stand together and say we have been wronged. It's harder to look at the ways that some of us have the power to wrong each other. If we mean to struggle as trusted equals, we have no choice but to speak this truth. And the good thing about telling the truth—not the problem, as I'd once thought—is that then we have to do something about it.

᚜◉᚛

FINDING AND MAKING THE REASONS

Sophie Pollitt-Cohen

———

$\mathcal{At}$ various points in my life I have been a closeted feminist, a frustrated feminist, and a starving feminist. Always, feminism has been bound up with appearance.

Until freshman year of college, I had been a secret feminist. I knew I believed in the ideas my mother—a well-known feminist writer—had brought me up with, but I did not want to use that word. To me feminism was based on obvious notions of equality: Women should have the same jobs as men, and jokes revolving around women being terrible drivers are sexist and also just lame. It seemed to me that by giving ourselves a title, we were saying that we were the only ones who needed to care about these issues. There is no special word for people who support civil rights and fair treatment of black people or gay people. Why do people that care about women's rights need a special word to band all of us freaks together?

So in my freshman-year introduction to sociology class, when the professor had us read an article by my mom and then asked us to raise our hands if we considered ourselves feminists, I didn't know what to do. I hesitated, ostensibly because the word seemed unnecessary. But really it was because I was afraid of being associated with a negative stereotype. I didn't want the cute boys in my class to think I hated them or was a lesbian or fat.

In reality, I had a boyfriend, was never romantically interested in females, and weighed ninety-nine pounds. But in my mind—because it had always been impossible for me to separate feminism from notions of beauty—the minute I raised my hand, I would transform right there in class. I would get hairy legs, I would gain twenty pounds, and my long hair would shrink back into my head. Then the boys wouldn't want to date me, and everyone would think I hated fun. I actually love fun, but I did not want people to think I would be a downer, always reminding everyone why they shouldn't like something—because it's *sexist*. (My mom does that a lot, but usually she's right.)

I did raise my hand, and I felt good about it. Plus, there was only one male lacrosse player in my class, so it wasn't that big a deal. After that, I embraced identifying as a feminist, setting nineteen years of my mother's fears to rest. That day ushered in a time of being excited to use a word that finally explained so many of my frustrations. I realized it is a special, specific word. It's more than just caring that women not be treated like dirt, or believing in basic, vague concepts of equality. It's taking it upon yourself to be aware of what you are involved in and what is going on around you.

For instance, watching TV became nearly impossible for me, but at least now I knew I wasn't the crazy one. Watching the Victoria's Secret fashion show on TV with my boyfriend and his friends made me want to offer someone personal violence, as Poe would say—why couldn't they understand that their cheering and detailed critiques of the models might offend the girls in the room? Why didn't they see that these models looked like seven-foot-tall little boys with implants? When watching *The Hills* on Monday nights, why didn't any of my friends say anything when we would see yet another commercial directed at women about eating healthy (except for Cheerios for lower cholesterol), losing weight, or cleaning something? Feminism has let me know that I'm not irrational and my mom isn't just annoying. We're feminists. And everyone else is stupid.

It turned out this kind of feminism was not enough when I joined the rugby team that fall, my sophomore year. I went from being afraid to be seen as too radical to a world in which I was perceived as too conservative. I wasn't feminist enough because I looked like a different stereotype—heteronormative.

Wesleyan women's rugby is a transinclusive team called WesRugby—our men's team, which is not transinclusive or associated with queer politics, is Old Methodist Rugby Football Club. The name WesRugby frustrated me. If I wore my Wes-Rugby shirt at home, people might assume I had borrowed it from a guy. I was proud to be a member of that team, because I was a female doing something physically demanding that most people wouldn't expect of any girl, and I felt the name diminished that. This was a conservative idea for a WesRugger.

The team is a safe space for queer people, and this is valuable and important. However, because I wasn't queer, I felt marginalized as a player. As a small, straight girl with long blond hair who liked wearing short dresses at parties and was dating the captain of the men's team (to be fair, think skinny Jewish boy from Jersey, not big WASP from wherever WASPs come from—that doesn't sound cliché if I make a joke about it), it seemed I wasn't a real feminist.

click

Frequently, if any of the straight players would kiss a queer player at a rugby party, she/ze would immediately be more socially included. More than once, I heard someone say that a straight player was "so much cooler now that she's gay." I felt excluded because I chose not to participate in that. Apparently, getting drunk and making out with a girl makes you queer. And yet, we never got to watch Girls Gone Wild during our pregame chalk talks.

Being on the team was an important learning experience. I was introduced to a slice of society that was new to me. Similarly, I was a window for some players into a weird world that they found interesting and amusing. At first, I embraced how different I was to have a place on the team. I wore pink cleats and told the team funny stories about the guys I was dating or hooking up with—the soccer player, the basketball captain, the lacrosse captain, the quarterback, the other lacrosse captain.

Soon I realized they weren't laughing with me so much as at me. Even though I was a decent player—albeit the most frequently injured on the team—I felt I wasn't taken seriously because I looked—and acted—too straight.

My teammates might have been onto something, though, because I soon found myself becoming exactly what they were talking about, a different kind of stereotype—a girl obsessed with her weight. My last season was the spring of my junior year, after having spent the fall abroad in Italy. By this point I had decided to opt out of most of the social aspects of the team. I ran and lifted weights in the mornings before class, tried my hardest at practice and at games, but did not spend time with the team between those activities.

I felt happier once I had stopped trying to socially fit in on the team, but I got a whole new fun complication. I focused my life on dieting, and I worried now that this meant I wasn't a real feminist. I knew I could be a feminist with long hair and pink cleats, but I wasn't sure if I could still be one who lived on seven hundred calories a day.

In Italy, I had decided to not exercise and to eat whatever I wanted. I figured this was probably the one time in my life when I would be able to do that, and I'm glad I did. Who would want to live in Italy around all that delicious food and not eat it? Some of the best times I had were cooking dinner with my host mom and teaching her English kitchen phrases, like to *run out* of sugar. I also discovered the wonders of Kono Pizza, which is basically like Subway, except instead of picking out sandwich toppings, you pick out pizza toppings, and instead of a pizza slice it's a pizza cone that they then put in an oven and you can drool and watch your Kono rotate around and around under the lights as it gets all crispy and beautiful.

Anyway, I'm not going to tell how much I gained in Italy, because I would prefer not to relive the experience. I will just say I came home and couldn't fit into my old jeans.

My whole life I had been skinny. Coming home with a new body was disturbing and scary. Growing up, my parents had only been concerned with my health—they had never put pressure on me to look a certain way. It was as I got older, and the influences of the outside world became stronger than those of my home, that I started worrying I wasn't thin enough. After twenty-one years of people telling me how little I was, I started to think that was the most important and interesting thing about me. A Sophie that was a size medium was not a Sophie. The four-month vacation was over, and I knew I needed to lose the weight I had gained.

First I sat on my bed and cried. Then I embarked on a mission to get back to my pre-pasta-party body. At most, I ate eight hundred calories a day. I went to the gym every morning, and I wrote down exactly what I ate and how many calories it contained. I cried a lot and was mean to my mother, because I was exhausted, frustrated, and hungry.

click

Eventually I did lose the weight, but it only made things slightly easier. The harshest reality of life is that you will never reach your goal weight, because your goal weight and current weight are directly proportional. In math we might say (GW ((CW. In English we say you will never be satisfied, and you will always feel fat. Also, it is nearly impossible to stop counting calories once you start. And once you know you can subsist on eight hundred calories a day, it continues to sound like a pretty nice number to try for even after you can fit into your pants. I'm much more normal now, but I don't think I know any girl who is completely "normal" about food.

Even though the rational part of my brain knows I am thin, I can't help but carry around the paranoia that most women my age do—that I will get fat if I eat that, drink that, don't get on the elliptical for forty minutes every day and then do circuit training. Dating someone who used this as a way to keep me from going out and meeting new boys did not help (parties have alcohol; alcohol has calories). I want to be a smart, aware feminist, but I don't know if you can be one if you buy into all the body and beauty standards.

I guess now I'm a make-it-up-as-I-go-along feminist. (Fun fact: I accidentally first typed "make-it-up-as-I-go-alone." If I were my own psychiatrist, I wouldn't even pay myself.) Now that I've quit the rugby team and I eat, my newest issue is getting dressed to go out at night. As I look at my clothes, my closet first becomes crowded with the boys I want to impress. They pull out my mini dresses and tell me *Soph, you would look so hot in this.* Which is true, but only my friends can call me Soph. Then WesRugby piles in, and they start asking me what it means to wear short dresses and high heels that I once thought were harmless. Aren't I reinforcing a reactionary position in society? Then my mom comes in and asks why I'm trying to impress these guys in the first place—are they really the ones who will be kind to me? Shouldn't I be interested in someone who is interested in my mind? By wearing these clothes, am I being asked not to be taken seriously, not to be asked about my opinions on Boswell and Johnson or sugar plantations? She also reminds me that heels are terrible for my feet. Then Thoreau and Emerson push everyone out of the way, and they stand on either side of me. *Listen, Soph, who makes your clothes?* Thoreau asks, leaning on my left shoulder. Emerson leans on my right and asks, *Also, what are you involved in here? You must not be too protected a person.* But then Ben Franklin comes in and points to his coonskin cap, and that's all he needs to do, because I know he means that sometimes you wear what others like to get what you want.

I kick everyone out of my closet, but I'm still confused. I like wearing things that show off my body. For most of my life—basically until I was nineteen—I looked like a little boy. Then *finally* I got boobs, and my hair figured itself out, and I actually thought I was pretty. I didn't want to start covering up what I was so newly excited about, but the clothes might be covering up another thing I was becoming passionate about— my new favorite authors. Mark Twain, Nathaniel Hawthorne, James Boswell, T. S. Eliot—all of these new friends were giving me a lot of new stuff to think about, ideas I was excited to share with my more twenty-first-century-inclined friends. It's made it difficult to pull all of this stuff together. I worry about finding a balance between striving to be relatively standard, heteronormative attractive, and not ignoring the awareness feminism has brought me. I worry that some of my more superficial interests and concerns make me less of a feminist.

I've come around to thinking that the ideas we feminists are concerned with are too important to be oversimplified. I do not think I should be kicked out of the club because I have a complex about being fat or because the boys I date (okay, love from afar) are varsity athletes, some of whom may or may not have dabbled in steroids. Feminism as a strict all-or-nothing

I Married a War Correspondent

Alissa Quart

About two years ago, I married a war correspondent. You are probably imagining that I myself am a war correspondent, an aid worker, or at least a human rights lawyer. If not, perhaps I am a woman known for being patient, calm, and unafraid of death, one who tastefully tends a shared apartment while my husband infiltrates overseas hellholes.

You would be wrong on all counts. Although I do write on American alternative culture, which sometimes contains the more metaphorical violence of social transgression, I tend to like abstract rather than blood-drenched ideas. I am interested in politics but domestic ones: the politics of youth and gender and race. The truth of the matter is that I've never been interested in conflict, except the kind that happens between two people that, hopefully, leads to their emotional growth.

click

That all changed, or at least came into question, when I first met my husband, at a party at a hotel bar in 2003. I noticed him across the room: His eyes were a beautiful, overly intense blue. He was very slim, with a shaved head and long neck. After we met, we stood near the bar's shimmering fire, gabbing without end.

We sealed our new bond when we went outside the hotel together and he lit a cigarette.

"I just started smoking," he confided.

"Bad love affair?" I asked.

"Bad war," he answered. He had been one of the first reporters in during the invasion of Iraq the previous April, he told me, and had covered conflict most of his life. Seeing I was shivering in the cold November air, he wrapped my shoulders with his jacket.

He was elegant and restrained. Given these qualities, I didn't have a clue he wrote on conflict zones and would soon return to Iraq yet again; had lived in a city under siege for a year; had walked around a Somali town with a warlord and met his many wives; and was one of few Westerners to have visited North Korea. He stood with troops in Iraq while they were fired upon. He drove through a minefield at night. And he was planning to go back to it all.

He had not spent his adult years snowing girls over Mojitos but rather driving on dirt roads trying not to be taken hostage. He was used to interrogating dictators and their henchmen, and as a result, he couldn't sweet-talk a woman like the rest of the sleek bachelors—those entrepreneurs of romance. The perpetual traveler was also a man married to his work. He hadn't refined a separate, private personality away from it.

It—our relationship, as it quickly developed—was lovely but disturbing. I had never planned to sit at the metaphorical feet of the would-be male genius, an "important" man. Yet despite myself, my resentment brought me closer to him. I left my favorite black corduroys and winter coat with the round wood buttons at his house. In short, we were in love. It all had me questioning—was I really a feminist?

I thought I was. But I had to wonder, for the first time, whether my feminism was merely a lazy inheritance. Maybe it had been simply handed down to me by my mother, who wrote for *Ms.* and only respected women who were professionally accomplished, who never once asked me about getting married or having children into my thirties.

I wasn't sure I had ever earned my stance with inquiry. There were my copies of Irigaray, god help me, and de Beauvoir. There was that once-watched DVD of feminist pornography (boring, unfortunately but predictably).

I fretted that all along, I had just been waiting for a Great Man to reveal me as charming but pointless. Had all of my years of aggressive intellectuality and gender play been mere self-delusion?

My boyfriend kept going on monthlong trips to increasingly dangerous places. The first was Moscow and Azerbaijan. During that three-week trip, I received only a small drizzle of emails and one phone call. I assumed that this silence meant something as petty as *we were no longer dating.*

But when he returned, he gave me a very special gift—a plaster bust of Vladimir Putin. A statue of the president of Russia isn't really the typical gift to one's lover. But coming from him, it was a profound totem of his love, along with the key chain of the dear leader of North Korea he would give me later and the rare pin of Saddam Hussein's visage I received on the week of our meeting. The next morning, he showed me a book of photos of war zones, pointing out places he had been while we sat in his apartment and I was simultaneously awed and irked.

click

Why wasn't his life my life? Why was I trapped in the city
while he really *lived*? And why had I chosen to be in the shadow of
a fellow whose "masculine" journalism—and politics—were given
more conventional props than my "feminine" interests? I wrote
on things like rotoscoping, self-branding, and amateurism. Yet
they never seemed important enough to me as compared to Kabul,
Basra, or Somalia.

Every so often, we would fight, usually before or after he
returned from a dangerous, lengthy trip that kept me focusing
on him. Does love exist? he'd ask. I got bored. He got selfish. I
jumped out of a slowly moving taxi and slammed the door—I
saw yellow all the way home. We broke up six times. I started
to feel like a histrionic twentysomething in a reality television
show. The first time was when he reported on a small African
dictatorship. At the airport, he was detained, led by armed
guards to a room where he called me on his cell phone. In that
conversation, he tried to sound like he was as relaxed as he was
when he was down at the local bakery. For twenty-four hours,
I waited to hear how he was as the guards threatened to take
away his passport. He only bothered to call me the next night,
from his hotel room in the next nation on that continent. He
was "Just fine. . . . "

Right.

Back home, I had nothing in the refrigerator besides a
bottle of dried plums and soymilk. I suddenly felt there was
nothing luminous about being lonely and underfed, waiting
for a boyfriend who was always away doing something even
more serious in the eyes of the world. It was diminishing. In
the morning I'd wander down for coffee and then I would work
straight through to evening, when I would break for drinks
with my few friends who were not yet pregnant. Was this really
what women in New York in their thirties were like—extras
in *Revolutionary Road*? How could I be so unfree? I had never
defined myself through the men I was with. And yet now, I was

suddenly overwhelmed by thoughts of his life (dazzling) and fear of his death (constant)? I felt like I was being neutralized, a victim of what could be called his "Masculine Mystique."

Of course, I had been attracted to him for my own reasons. I liked to feel as if I were part of a chronicle, something larger and worldlier than myself, as I was in my childhood. As a lonesome, imaginative kid I memorized atlases and encyclopedias for the imports and exports of countries I would never go to and wanted more than anything to visit: Antarctica, the Ecuadorian rain forest. Yet as an adult, I'd never had the physical confidence to go to the Congo. My boyfriend became my living atlas, and I continued to sit alone in a high-backed chair, turning the proverbial pages of his life.

Yet when I thought of the future, I wondered: What if I lived through him for the rest of my life? It seemed unbearable.

His worst trip by far was the last month he spent in Iraq, in 2005. At first, he didn't tell me where he was going or what he was writing about. One day, he was packing his satellite phone and flak jacket, and the next he was in Baghdad and then Samara. He made my job—worrying—harder by dissembling about where he was going and how much danger he would be in once he arrived. Lying was a tactic he'd refined on his family. With them, he had gotten away with it.

With me, not as much. In Falluja, Samara, and Baghdad at the time, there were frequent civilian bombings. I sent emails just as frequently. And he replied infrequently, with few words. He'd call occasionally from his satellite phone, after reporting on some night raid or other, his voice patchy and scratchy. Why was I accepting this? I wondered. It sounded as if the sand around him had actually made its way into the receiver.

I checked the Web constantly for news of attacks. At night, I would go out and drink that second glass of wine, take a taxi home that was too expensive for my bank account, and stumble the five stories of stairs to my apartment, where I'd fall asleep dressed, with the lights on, hoping he'd call to tell me he was fine. Meanwhile, he would be in a vehicle leaving the Green Zone or going out on raids for high value targets, walking in detention centers covered with bloodstains and listening to human screams. I felt corny and girlish, like a single female character in a play from the 1980s, thinking: *I just want someone to laugh with!*

But here's the thing. Rather than breaking up with him this time, I actually *moved into his apartment* while he was away. I told myself I did it so I could be near his things, and that was partially true. Like a woman in a cologne ad from the 1970s, I went through his closets, trying on his shirts, attempting to be as close to him as possible. And he must have had the same idea, for when he returned from a trip to Iraq, just in time for my thirty-third birthday, he was carrying a ring he had purchased in Baghdad. It was a man's ring: beautiful and multicolored, comically big for my hands.

I didn't say "yes" for the entire year. It was more than the fact that the ring didn't fit. I was afraid to continue living in his public shadow. How could a woman like me not want a partner who was, well, *around?* And to make things worse, he wanted me to cook! How could I, of all people, be rendered a household saint?

The truth was, I couldn't. I *had* to, to put it cornily, "choose" myself. This was certainly a feminist moment. It was the moment when I stopped trying things on and made choices that had to do with a core truth, as they say in self-help, that I hadn't yet fully defined. As Betty Friedan wrote, "the only kind of work which permits an able woman to realize her abilities fully is the kind that was forbidden by the feminine mystique, the lifelong commitment to art or science, to politics or profession." I had to commit myself to this kind of work, and believe it was at least as important as his.

But one day, eight months into our long nonengagement,

he told me he was not going to go to active war zones. He was still going on long reporting trips or to places that were dangerous by any sane person's reckoning (cue cars driving backward in the rain on a dirt road in a West African country). But at least he wasn't going to die by an improvised explosive device. He was also not just making this sacrifice for me. He was choosing it for himself. And I felt that I could marry him (though, you know, I didn't really approve of marriage).

On the midsummer night close to three years ago, with friends looking on, we were married on the grounds of an Adirondack estate. It was one of the best days of both of our lives and as exciting, I think, as any reporting trip in an exotic locale. We even honored his years in the Balkans with a Bulgarian DJ. The guests drank Bloody Marys on a glamorously run-down wraparound porch with wildflowers in Adirondack baskets. The wedding photographer was also a war photographer—she had just gotten back from taking pictures of an uprising in the Philippines.

In the years since our marriage, we have edged toward one another. We spend much of our time together, a first for both of us—ragged iconoclasts who have finally hewn to another. Yet even together, our understanding of ordinary life is still somewhat impaired. We still do not own a Cuisinart, both find "couple's dinners" hard to bear, and have for years written our books side by side, even at nighttime and on vacation. And I have also finally fully taken in what all the female writers I had ever read and loved have written so well about. Photography or urban planning or gender, and, of course, ordinary women and children, and interpreting them, can also be great works. They can be as searing, in their way, as investigating bullets, presidents, and dictators.

Righteous Little Beaver

Amy Richards

———

In my junior year of college I joined a rather snobby and exclusive coed fraternity. I was delighted to be asked but a bit mortified by the prospect of actually having to accept. Ninety-nine percent of the appeal was being chosen, giving me the ultimate power to accept or reject. Part of the pledging process was being assigned a nickname. Mine: righteous little beaver. Some friends were offended on my behalf, but I was *kinda* flattered. This description meshed with my image of myself as an outspoken, stubborn activist committed to uprooting injustices and changing the world—though I think I was probably more docile—at least complacent—than I ever gave off. But I felt understood; the preppy upper-class boys seemed to get me after all.

This reputation stayed with me as a good summation of my undergraduate years. Besides getting a rigorous education and indulging the debaucherous aspects of college, I was trying out different identities and fine-tuning some opinions that had resonated with me, but which I hadn't entirely formulated, such as what it meant to be marginalized or oppressed or what privilege was. I intentionally began incorporating activism into my daily life: I traveled to Washington DC to march with Bread and Roses Puppet Theater to oppose the first Gulf War and later to chant in front of the White House "Free Barbara's Bush," alluding to George senior's anti-abortion stance silencing his wife's more pro-choice instincts. I protested against my rich university for not paying secretaries a living wage and for selling the historic theater where Malcolm X was killed to someone promising to turn it into a medical waste incinerator. I marched in my college's annual Take Back the Night. I was asking out loud: Why had Planned Parenthood been the only healthcare provider offering affordable birth control? How could the Los Angeles Police officers be found not guilty of beating Rodney King when the entire thing was caught on video? Like many college students, I was learning to challenge the status quo and beginning to realize my power.

Political activism wasn't new to me but was more a crescendo of a life committed to making observations and speaking out. When I was barely cognizant I was exposed to the fact that life wasn't fair, that some people had it easier than others, and that some people had strong opinions that stood in the way of others' being free. It all began with being born to a single mother who was also an outspoken feminist—one who challenged my love of Barbies and hung around with her women's group talking about the latest issue of Ms. magazine. She encouraged me to be a congressional page when it was still a boys' club and encouraged my athleticism. But besides her actualized feminist self, my mother's main draw to feminism was a consequence of desperation, not choice. My mother had conceived me in the context of her marriage to my father, but seven months pregnant with me she realized that he was not enrolled in medical school, as he had told her, and that unleashed a dozen more lies. Thank goodness she had the chutzpah to leave—despite the advice she got from most people: "Keep your marriage together at all costs." In hindsight, I realize this advice wasn't based so much on an utter belief in convention, but on survival—being a single mother in 1970 was not a powerful place to be. But luckily my mother acted on her good instincts.

Though being a feminist crusader seems an obvious lifestyle choice for me, part of my DNA, it was only after my bratty teenage years that I warmed to the importance of women's equality. Not coincidentally it was around this same time that I realized that being a vegetarian was cool, a value my mother had also previously tried to instill in me by making her own hummus and joining a food co-op. (Moral of my story: Always listen to your mother.) But to be fully convinced of the importance of this movement, I needed the feminism to be mine, not my mother's; I needed a nonfamiliar confirmation that feminism was something positive, not simply a desperate or hippie place.

During college I started taking cues from professors and peers I admired and—most memorably—from a hard-ass powerful lawyer specializing in divorce and custody who I worked for over the course of three years; she put the fear of god into those who made life difficult for her clients. Deep down she was a pussycat, which is why most of her clients wanted her and why an impressionable young woman like me wanted to be her. For her generation, she had done the "right" thing: She graduated from Radcliffe, married well, and had three boys. Then, in her forties, her husband left her. She went to law school and went on to create a very respected firm. Her confidence was starting to feel familiar—one friend in college was barely twenty and had already traveled around most of Africa and Latin America with her mother, helping women get access to safe birth control. She knew women were being wronged and was already committed to correcting these injustices. These people made

click

feminism appealing—and seemingly the only lifestyle choice for a self-respecting, ambitious young woman like me.

Bolstered by their examples, I started paying more attention to what angered me and how I might be able to change it. In the spring of my senior year, a few people were hosting a meeting about how to reverse the political apathy among younger women. I went to the meeting and, at the end of the two hours, found myself in the midst of creating what would become Freedom Summer '92, a cross-country voter registration drive where a handful of us organized to take 120, primarily young, people on three buses across the country to register voters in poor communities like East St. Louis, Illinois, and Greenville, Mississippi. We were emboldened by a sense that people deserved "more," a better quality of life, and that our country needed to hear from all its citizens. I put in twenty-hour days because I assumed the culmination of my work would make a dent in making the world a better place "for others"; in this instance, those who didn't have ready access to speaking up or to a political platform, those who had been told that they couldn't vote because they were too old, too poor, or *too* black. I wanted to help those who were "oppressed" and underserved.

Then it *clicked*—wait a minute, if I live in a country that isn't living up to its promise of democracy, that's doing a disservice to me, too. I was standing on the streets of Philadelphia simultaneously registering voters, feeling overwhelmed that I had only registered two voters in nine hours, and high on the fact that I was a good person for giving myself to "the cause." But I had to ask—was I doing this for "me" or for "them"? My investment had to be greater than helping those in need. This acknowledgment of universal oppression evolved my thinking. We all experience discrimination in different ways, certainly some more severely and less naively than others, but living in a world where anyone is oppressed hinders everyone.

While I was stationed outside supermarkets and in lines

at unemployment offices trying to convince people that voting was in their best interest, I noticed something else— women were the poorest of the poor, and it was only women who would say something to the effect of "hurry and register me before my husband comes back," alluding to their "kept woman" status. I tried to inspire people to register to vote by making a connection to local issues—such as tearing down a neighborhood to build highways or the cost of healthcare. I realized that it was often women who had the most to gain or lose, depending on the issues—when it came to cutting public benefits, women would be the most penalized; when it came to creating a livable wage campaign, women's salaries had the most to gain.

Like many of those of my generation, I eased into feminism after first trying out other social justice movements—civil rights and examining class and economic oppressions. Feminism has a history of being born of other movements—the abolitionists preceded the suffragists; the peaceniks preceded the women's libbers. But uniquely for me, and for most of my peers, feminism was a given—we played sports, said we could be anything, and occasionally even treated our dates. How much we were willing to acknowledge and deepen that awareness was the barometer of the ultimate conversion. It wasn't a matter of living with feminist principles, but how much we were willing to claim the feminist label.

After my final capitulations that I really was a feminist, I had to ask, *What had I really been so scared of?* I could handle being called a man-hating hairy lesbian—partly because I was pretty confidently straight and hairy by choice, mostly trying to disassociate from every other WASP-looking girl. Reflecting back, I think I was most fearful of having to acknowledge my own limitations. I wasn't really ready to own the power I was advocating for.

As punishing as the invisibility was for women of another

era, being visible was proving to be hard work. I also assumed that if I identified so publicly with this movement, people would know that I had had an abortion or that I had been raped. I was scared about how much my politics would expose my personal life. But then I realized that the only way to stop feeling badly about things that happened to me, and that I observed happening to others, was to change the assumption that some people were "problem-free." It was a gradual acknowledgment that the very things that seemingly made me vulnerable were what made me who I am. Certainly we don't want people to unnecessarily suffer, but learning to persevere and work with difference often strengthens us. Rarely is it the "thing" itself that is so traumatic (be it rape, racism, or slut-bashing), but how others responded to our situation—how much support we did or didn't get.

My journey feels far from complete. I still have almost daily moments where I say, "I can't believe I didn't know that. . . . " That's the exact point of the click; you don't go back, your thinking only progresses. Today I am likely to help usher in other people's clicks. I lecture on college campuses, and students tell me how concerned they are for the women in Iran or the women in the Congo; others will relate that while they are certainly motivated to want to do more in the name of equality, they personally haven't experienced discrimination. They get that women are suffering, but it's usually "other" women. Their journeys seem reminiscent of what I learned all those years ago: personal stake. I'm sympathetic to these excuses—I hear them out, and if I ever have more than a moment, I try to relay my own journey. We think it's about others, but it's really about us.

While I was initially trying to depersonalize the politics, I later realized how important it is to remind ourselves how deeply personal social justice work must be. Case in point: People will often ask me how I can stand to be on Bill O'Reilly's notoriously conservative *The O'Reilly Factor,* which I have done a few times—but it's actually pretty easy to disagree with a right-wing ideologue and have him tell me that I am scum. It's harder to have friends say some version of "why are you always so politically correct?" Trivializing or discounting the personal investment in our political beliefs is precisely why we haven't made more progress. We have to believe it to truly fight for it.

How funny that all these years after proudly owning my righteous beaver description, I would learn that beavers swim upstream to protect themselves and their dams, which is exactly what feminists have to do. I initially didn't see this struggle and resistance as a positive for feminism. I wanted the movement to be easier, more popular, and less precarious, but now I see that the struggle is what makes it feminist—not willingly tolerating what society has said is the rule. Being righteous might not be the most flattering compliment, but without that utter belief that we are doing the right thing we won't progress.

~∾~

THE FEMINIST EVOLUTION OF AN ARTIST, SURVIVOR, CONJURER FROM THE TROPICS

Marta L. Sanchez

⟶

I became a feminist at creation, not at birth, but between conception and the light. Feminism named me, while my grandfather strung binding words together beneath a tree. My father nurtured me a feminist. I was a feminist when I was raped on my way to Paradise. I was a feminist when I worked at the Feminist Women's Health Center in Atlanta, shedding light on my own abortion experience. I was a feminist the day I became an artist, fell in love, and every day that activism guides me through this world.

I grew up in the Republic of Panama, where palm tree fronds conspire with tropical breeze to mock the thunderous sound of rain. I was sun-kissed every day, and the ocean framed my world. I was nurtured into feminism by my parents, my Panamanian father and my African American mother.

My mother loved to tell this story, recounting my coming into being like a sculptor describing her work, "Baby," she would say, "when I was pregnant with you, I thought about your eyes, and I thought about your skin. I imagined what your lips would look like, your ears, your eyes, and your hands. I focused on each part of you and envisioned it, just so. And you came out just the way I saw it. You came out perfect. . . . Except baby, I'm sorry, I forgot about your feet."

Feminism involves a great deal of sculpting. It relies on the notion that the reality that we live is not the way things must be, or the way they have always been. In feminism I find a duty to dream, to pay attention to each small detail as I envision what I want. I believe that I can change things, and that anything I can focus on can come into being.

When I was born I was named after two powerful feminists. My grandmother Martha was strong: strong willed, strong spirited, strong voiced. Her words carried, in sayings like, "Beauty is as beauty does." Although I cannot remember many things she did, photos tell me she was movie star beautiful. My mother tells me my grandmother was deeply intelligent but never finished the eighth grade. She lived surrounded by people with degrees.

Now, I can trace a few things up my mother's line. A nagging feeling that I should hide at least some of my money from my husband (*always keep a secret stash in case you have to get away*). A strong impulse to get the best education I can so I have options and no one can force me to work a job I don't want. Most strikingly, I inherited the belief that I should look good (keep my calm, maintain appearances, and pretend all is well), even if I feel bad. And never forget that proper manners go a long way.

I can't tell you whether my mom has large sums of money

hidden away without severe consequences, but I can openly credit Martha's strong will with my mother's PhD and my law degree. I can also blame her for my mother's torturous obsession with Ms. Manners. I keenly know how to put up a good front when I am down. My ability to keep my cool through hardship is probably why years went by and only the fistful of people I confided in knew I was a survivor.

My other namesake may have rescued me from silence. My Aunt Laura was my father's favorite sister. Although I never met her, I hear she lived life rebelliously. In a location and time when it was unheard of Laura, a single woman, moved into her own place. There she went to sleep late, woke up late, owned a small business, and enjoyed life to the fullest. We never met. She died at thirty-four.

I often wonder how much names dictate perspectives and behavior. At times, I feel Martha and Laura struggling within. Martha is the part of me that is proper, dignified, plays by the rules, and prepares for every possible crisis. She is cool, perfect for emergencies. She always looks good. Laura is the part of me that is playfully wild. She could care less what others think and keeps no secrets. She treasures each moment, roams free of imposed schedules. An entrepreneur, she will never live under anyone's rule or dominance.

These names, filled with strength of will, were passed down to me, along with certain cultural beliefs that I rejected. When I was about four, the age when people speak openly and expect that you will forget every word, Grandpa Wes (provoked by some event I cannot recall) informed me that "Pretty girls don't like other pretty girls."

Even then, I was stubborn, and searched for ways to prove my point to the extreme. Now, I can't remember ever having had a friend who was not flat-out gorgeous. Later, I realized my rejecting this notion went against our society's push to divide and conquer, to create women who are catty, jealous, and self-involved. Is it beauty contests that leave us feeling that there can only be one winner, one true beauty?

My grandfather's words led me to focus on the way women are taught to isolate one another, instead of providing mutual support. I chose to reject those words asserted as truth, although they could have hung around my neck like a noose, cutting off the inspiration and light I gain from my ties with beautiful, strong women around me.

While I embraced a belief in solidarity, I still experienced the isolation imposed by gossip. It was what kept me silent after being raped. A girl assaulted in the same community was scrutinized and criticized to a level I was unwilling to endure. This major life event, being raped at sixteen, instantly made me a feminist. I could no longer blame the victim. I could no longer believe that rape was provoked by what we wear or what we do. I had done everything "right." I knew him. He was at least six years older than me. He offered me a ride to church, a day or two before Christmas, 1994, in a town called Paraiso, which means Paradise.

I stopped speaking to the god my church loved, suddenly turned off by his being male, moody, judgmental, unforgiving, and (apparently) unavailable to protect sixteen-year-olds who accept rides to his place.

Most jarringly, I found myself disconnected afterward. Sometime after he started raping me I found myself floating above my body. This led me to understand why rape is not about sex, why it is a crime of power and control, and how the true harm in rape is that it is an eviction of spirit. It is a traumatic dictatorship imposed on your body, the one thing that should be guaranteed yours for life.

Besides detachment from my body, I have had to learn to process other consequences of the rape. Sometimes, it is hard for me to keep the positive in focus, to acknowledge that I am okay now, and there have always been many wonderful things and people in my life.

My dad, for example, who deliberately raised me to be a feminist. He is a sensitive guy disguised as a serious engineer, unafraid of (or maybe accustomed to) surrounding himself by strong women. Growing up, I remember people in my neighborhood being afraid of him, especially the boys. They would somehow miss that he is gentle and kind, the type of guy small children and animals wander up to, fearlessly.

He taught me to play tennis and, through the game, instilled certain values: Keep your eye on the ball, everything worth achieving takes work, and spend time with the ones you love. The most important things he affirmed were my right to question everything, and my right to have a healthy, respectful, and loving relationship with a good man. We were always very close, talking every day, up until I left Panama in 1996, to attend Spelman College in Atlanta.

At Spelman, I became a women's studies major. Suddenly, the entire world made sense. I stopped feeling like an alien visiting a strange planet. I thrived as I explored the new information within my reach. I learned history from different perspectives, gaining access to the past as experienced by women, people of color, and LGBQT communities. I explored how society constructs gender, race, and class. Moments that stand out are the day I learned that there are five sexes not two. The stunning silence in the room the day one professor asked us if we realized we wouldn't all get married. The time we were asked if we thought a slave woman had ever had a bad hair day. The gentle guidance that followed, exploring how our perception of the black women in *The Cosby Show* made us feel that we had to become superwomen, beyond human sensitivities. (Mama Huxtable had a cold, what? Once? And she still managed to do everything that day.)

Most important, my women's studies classes exploring violence helped me reconcile and name my past experiences. Classes like Images of Women in the Media helped guide me toward art and visual expression as a means of processing my experiences.

After I graduated from college, I worked for a for-profit company that paid well and required little (torture). I left to work at a rape crisis center that paid less and demanded more (enlightening).

People would respond, "Wow, that sounds hard," when I told them about work. I always thought the most difficult role was the survivors'. *They* were resilient. If they could get up the nerve to go to the hospital to have a rape kit done right after an assault, I figured I could at least be there to support them.

Amazingly, that was not the hardest job of my life. Later, I was a counselor at the Feminist Women's Health Center (FWHC). Of all my experiences, it may be what most defined me as a feminist. It was amazing to be part of an organization that provides women with information, empowers their choices, and treats them like capable human beings.

This approach was why working at the FWHC was more demanding than working at the rape crisis center (in part as a support just after the assault). After a rape the survivor is focused on this one event, and how to move past it. Before an abortion, women are facing the entire circumstance of their lives. They are reviewing their emotional, financial, family, work, and home situation to decide if these are the ideal, or at least minimum, circumstances necessary to support a child. That analysis is overwhelming, and I can remember the smell of salt tears that often mingled with their words.

I knew I was a feminist then, because it affirmed my belief in a woman's right to choose, because as a witness to their process I observed the careful consideration of the issues, heard them muse out loud. I saw their clarity and intelligence. It confirmed my belief that women are wise beings, and that the individual in the difficult position (be it a rape or an unplanned pregnancy) is most qualified to pinpoint all the consequences and make the best choice.

Moreover, the way the FWHC approached abortion stood starkly against my personal experience with abortion. In 1994, when I was assaulted, I became pregnant. Each night that followed, I dreamed of an angel bringing me a child to protect. When the pregnancy was discovered, my mother made an appointment for me to have an abortion. I was flown to Miami, and put under anesthesia. The procedure was performed. To her credit, the nurse working at the clinic did say to me, "No one can force you to have an abortion; it's your choice," but at sixteen, I did not feel I had choices. I remember thinking: *And who am I going to live with? You?*

And to her credit, when I woke up to the sound of a woman screaming at the top of her lungs for her baby and slowly discovered the woman was me, and I had explained the entire situation, from conception up to the present moment, to this nurse, she insisted that I tell someone. And that was how my mom found out I had been raped. I was drugged, groggy, and deeply in pain (physically and emotionally).

Somehow, I think that loss was more difficult to bear than the loss of self I experienced after being raped. Years went by before I stopped counting how old my baby would be. A decade slid by before I could hold a baby without wanting to cry.

And while some might think that this experience should have led me to stand on the other side (to be against choice and to work to ban abortion), what it left me with was a clear sense that this was my choice to be had, my decision to be made. I am pro-choice because were there less stigma and more information, there would be fewer abortions.

I knew this because I could see how misinformation had played a role in my life. Having attended a Catholic high school and junior high, I was convinced, going in, that abortion was dangerous and, in all likelihood, I would die on the table. Being raped had left me suicidal, and so I thought an abortion would conveniently kill me.

Working at the FWHC put me face-to-face with how things could have been. They gave each woman detailed information and counseling before an abortion. Informed women about the side effects and percentage of deaths associated with the procedure. (In a clinical setting it is an extremely safe, outpatient procedure. More women die in childbirth.) They had specific questions that were structured to detect any ambivalence on the woman's part. They made sure women had the self-care skills and the necessary support system afterward. They went beyond the goal of empowering women to make the most difficult decision of their lives and minimized the need for abortion. They offered sexual education, low cost birth control, and free information and support by phone.

This is the empowered world I wish I had had access to. Looking back I can't say I would have made a different decision if allowed a choice. I have, however, seen the difference between having an abortion you chose, felt empowered to have, armed with the resources to process the experience, and having an abortion that is imposed, unsupported, and/or shameful.

Because of my work at the crisis center and the FWHC, I discovered these decisions don't have to be made alone. The healing required does not have to be a solitary process.

Now, I am no longer alone. Beyond the beautiful community of women/sisters I have gathered, I can thank my feminist ancestors on both sides for bringing me love. On Martha's side we are sculptors, using words to create what we most want, conjuring it up like a baby in the womb of our minds.

My love list "My partner will be . . . " was three pages long. It had been constantly edited, revisited, and then abandoned due to the unlikelihood of finding (in summary) a guy who was smart, honest, open, emotionally available, beautiful, reliable, with great teeth, interested in the many things I love.

He was my list and showed up in the most unexpected time and place (while I was vacationing at home). We discovered that his family and my father's family had known each other for three generations. Ten days after we met we were legally married. Four days later we had a spiritual ceremony, led by a *reverenda* on the beach, while the sun rose and groups of tall white birds bore witness from the ocean.

Two and a half years have passed since that moment, and it remains one of the best decisions I ever made. Cleveland, like my father, is the kind of person that babies and small animals wander up to. He is sweetness, light, sincerity, and joy, bundled up into one tall package. His father is a dentist.

I was a feminist the day I fell in love with him. His kind responses when I told him I was a survivor were perfect. I knew he was the one because instead of reacting with the fear or criticalness that I'd experienced in the past (*You aren't going to flip out on me are you?* or *I don't understand why you didn't tell anyone*), when I told him I had been raped, he said, "I'm sorry that happened to you. It wasn't your fault. That should never happen," and he listened. Cleveland did not treat me like a flawed being meriting a straitjacket (*You should get help*). He treated me like a powerful being, one capable of sorting through her feelings through her creativity and her own unique process.

The truth is, I was a feminist the moment I started painting to express the feelings that resulted from the rape. Silence is difficult to break, so I created safe space. It was often canvas bound, drenched with color, vibrancy, and safety. I found empowerment on paper, sketching and writing. I let my words pour out, freeing my feelings from judgment-imposed exile. After a few years, I began using my art and experiences to educate, empowering communities to address sexual violence.

Now, every day feminism lives in me. I find more reasons

to be a feminist. I work for equality in all aspects of life, respect for people of all backgrounds, to empower others to envision the world they want. Feminism guides me to balance and positive change. It nontraditionally structures my relationship with my husband. We share the burden of living. Cleveland washes the clothes. I cook the food. I clean the house. He cleans the dishes. He irons. I am the fix-it-woman.

My life is magical because feminism has empowered me to live creatively, envision the love I want, the life I want, to be true to my voice. It has taught me the importance of information, education, and choice. It has led me to fake it sometimes when I need to, but in balance I learned to always be prepared, to use outward calm as a buffer zone in which to work on myself. Now I address things, with the help of beautiful friends, rather than bottling them up.

Feminism is an aqua green coat of ocean just under my skin, a bright light in my heart as I walk this earth as an activist. I deeply enjoy finding new ways to reach and embrace other feminists, like you.

∾∾

"What's the Female Version of a Hustler?": Womanist Training for a Bronx Nerd

Joshunda Sanders

The Bronx I grew up in used to be known as the least desirable place to live in New York. The bravado of its residents was augmented by dumb courage as young people were swept up in and changed by the crack cocaine economy, culture, and epidemic. Corners buzzed with clusters of mostly male teenage drug dealers, power lines sagged under the weight of old sneakers, empty crack vials littered the dirty concrete. Nature in the Bronx was a patch of four trees every two miles along Southern Boulevard, in parks with cracked green benches where syringes and broken Colt 45 bottles lingered in the grass.

As a result, girls from the Boogie Down had to be, in the streets, as welcoming as a brick house with broken windows and, behind closed doors with their boo, more pliant and ladylike. For poor black women like me, requiring parity like a feminist would have been a moot point. Black men had no real power to aspire to, other than the power brokered by invisible men who dropped omnipresent drugs on our streets. We womanists in training had to be more like partners to our men and to each other, hoodrats willing to weave razor blades into our extensions or scar a girl for life with nails laced with fresh garlic.

What I thought I knew about being a woman emerged from this limited, broken-down worldview, a perspective I believed was that of a serious grownup for at least a few years.

The story I told myself as a preteen was that despite whatever I would be called, if I was going to survive the Bronx or the world, I had to be as manly as or more so than the men I knew, those same men who sold drugs or carried unlicensed weapons or worse. I did not allow myself to believe I had a choice to be weaker, or feminine, as I thought of women who had the luxury of deciding not to be fighters because they did not live in drug war zones.

I have loved stories since I was a little girl. I ordered florid romances by mail and stole Sweet Valley High books from the Doubleday bookstore on Fifth Avenue. Before I knew better, the stories I enjoyed were mostly escapist literature for me: tales of white women that involved lounging in bikinis, or falling in love, or doing what they wanted. This was novel to me. I did what was in front of me, what was accessible. Black girls did not lounge by Crotona Pool, for example, where the water was shallow and there were likely to be dirty needles around. In the inner city, relaxation was not an option.

Still, in seventh grade, when I was a skinny, introverted girl who checked out piles of books from the New York Public Library, I read everything from academics bell hooks and Cornel West to Jackie Collins's Lucky series. I believed some ver-

sion of a plentiful, intellectual life was possible, but it looked .
. . white. My private junior high school was full of black nerds
just like me, so I felt encouraged. Then we all graduated, and
my closest friends went off to boarding school, where financial
aid and academic scholarships had catapulted them.

Without either of those things, I was left behind, without a supportive intellectual community and as a freshman at
Aquinas, an all-girl's Catholic school in the 'hood. Like many
of my classmates, I found the classes were too easy. Instead of
studying, I decided to shut down emotionally, to become the
meanest chick ever. Specifically, I wanted to be a Gangster
Bitch, like the Apache rap song of the same name.

I started dating John, who was a few years older than me
and worked in the locker room at the Boys and Girls Club
where I went after school with my homegirl, Lanell. After
work, he and his friends would rap outside of his apartment
building a couple of times a week. This inspired me to start
writing my own raps. One day, John asked me to spit a rhyme
for him. After he heard it, he was so excited that he deemed
me Lady Raw and Intelligent.

The foul, aggressive language part was effortless, but my
look left a little to be desired. I was frail, with fake braids and
big feet with no money to buy anything but men's shoes. I was
way too self-conscious for my career to ever have taken off.

More important, however, was that my heart wanted something different, something that seemed impossible. I wanted
to be a writer, but I thought that dream was impractical and
definitely out of my reach.

The writers I emulated were black women like Audre
Lorde, Nikki Giovanni, Zora Neale Hurston, and Alice
Walker, but none of them had come from where I had come
from. They were also years older than me, and in my genera-
tion, black girls who were smart got teased and beat up for it
(I was tossed into a Dumpster in the schoolyard of C.S. 67,

for instance, after getting a 100 on too many spelling tests).
How, I thought, would I get from the trash bins of the Bronx to
bookstores like Doubleday on Fifth Avenue? Besides, it seemed
uppity, to John and his friends and later, to me, to think that to
be a real writer, I needed to write essays or books.

In my generation, I would need to become a rapper. It required courage as a brute-force decision, one that looked brave,
like the rest of the women and men in my 'hood. I was striving for some kind of mediocrity, some way to fit in with what I
was supposed to become instead of alienating myself from my
friends, my homeboys, and yes, my man.

Some of my decision was informed by race. Rapping was black
and Latino, born in the Bronx. Writing? There was blackness in
it, but comparing the two was like comparing purple to lavender.
Later, when I would read a definition of womanism, I would see
the comparison clearly, understanding why I didn't believe I could
ever be a real rapper and a true, honest writer. In the meantime, I
struggled for street credibility.

I wrote all kinds of profanity, lyrics about fucking and
knocking hoes out. I couldn't even freestyle because it
made me stutter. Needless to say, my rapping career was
mercifully short.

What it taught me, though, was that I needed my own
authentic voice, one that resonated as much as that of any man
I'd encountered in the Bronx, but I didn't want to be considered masculine. I wanted to claim feminism, but I have always
cringed at the word.

Feminine terms are slightly foreign to me, since I have
lived with euphemisms for "strong black woman" all my life.
I am the kind of beautiful that arises from being unclassi-
cally interesting to look at and "exotic" as opposed to, say,
a "real woman" like, (name the white woman here). I have
been called every version of *scary* a black woman can be
called: "intimidating," "aggressive," or "striking." I can-

not recall ever being called "elegant" or "pretty" by anyone except my mother.

And when I applied to boarding school, a world of feminists, I started reading Alice Walker's work more. I found *In Search of Our Mothers' Gardens* at the library before I went off to boarding school. It included a definition of *womanism* that I instantly connected with:

Womanist: 1. *From the black folk expression of mothers to female children, "You acting womanish," i.e., like a woman. Usually referring to outrageous, audacious, courageous or willful behavior. Wanting to know more and in greater depth than is considered "good" for one. Interested in grown-up doings. Acting grown up. Being grown up. . . .*

It made me think of the feminists I had encountered. Mostly on television or in books. Feminism, to me, was a Manhattan brand of freedom. Being valued as a feminist required cash, a fly crib in a borough where people mattered, and a sense of entitlement. I had nothing but pride, and no time to be pissed off at John or any man who appreciated me as I was when the rest of the world—a world, in fact, that included feminists—ignored me.

But I also have always loved words and wrangling with sentences more than bravado; essays and thoughtful styling more than lyrical barbs. In the rap game, with all of its posturing, I was being more of a girl, not a woman. I was immature, regressing by embodying the stereotypes others had threatened to render me invisible; Walker's definition of womanism revised a space for me in a larger worldly context. I had believed, as a rapper, that to be like feminists, I had to be a woman who was equal to or even more aggressive than any man.

It sounds stupid now, even as I admit it to myself, but that's the problem with youth. You have lots of energy and time to come up with half-baked theories about things but not a lick of sense to really make it all come together. Thankfully, the second time I applied to boarding school, I got in. When I left the Bronx, when I was around more white women who more frequently used the word *feminism*, I carved out in my mind a space for myself as a newly branded womanist.

I stopped rapping and started to sing, this time as a hobby, and this time, it was songs written by bands like Extreme and the Indigo Girls. Claiming my voice gave me room to write, which I've been doing passionately ever since.

Most women don't use the word *womanist*; as a journalist, writer, and bookworm who reads avidly, I have yet to see the word enter mainstream discourse on a consistent basis. Not that it matters. As Sandy Banks, a writer for the *Los Angeles Times*, wrote in April, the newest generation of would-be feminists or womanists is the beneficiary of the work of women before us. "But it's more than a question of terminology," she wrote. "It's the evolution of a movement that succeeds by making itself obsolete."

Within the structure of womanism, which emerged from black culture, I went from being unable to relate to a world of Bella Abzugs or Gloria Steinems to seeing, in Alice Walker's definition, where Gloria, Bella, and Audre Lorde and Barbara Smith and Pat Parker all existed along a continuum. Because, indeed, some of us are brave, as one womanist text points out, I envisioned myself courageous, someone who could both refuse to choose between race loyalty and gender loyalty while being serious about my work, serious about being grown-up, purple, proud, and beautiful—Bronx beginnings and all.

YOU CAN'T RAPE A WHORE:
A LOVE STORY

Rachel Shukert

⌒

When I heard the news that Kurt Cobain had died, I was in the least rock-and-roll place imaginable: in the Nebraska state finals of the annual National Geographic National Geography Bee.

Everything about the event—the redundant awkwardness of its name, the plastic nametags we were required to pin to our unfashionably stiff official T-shirts, the squads of attending social studies teachers nervously dabbing at their dampening underarms with clumps of yellowing Kleenex—reeked with blatant uncoolness. I am a competitive person, but as an eighth-grader I was also excruciatingly self-conscious about such things. So when I was knocked out in the afternoon round by a possibly autistic Future Farmer of America with truly terrifying knowledge of plate tectonics in the Java Sea, my failure came as a massive relief. By the time I had made my way off the stage it was well past three o'clock, so I called my friend Sam from a pay phone in the lobby to catch up on the news of the day. Through tears, she told me that the tortured voice of our generation had been found dead on the floor of his house on Lake Washington by an electrician come to install a new security system. The cold gun was still pointing toward his chin. The coroner estimated that he had lain there undiscovered for more than three days.

I held the receiver by my side for a few moments, catching my breath. A gale of applause echoed from the auditorium as my bespectacled rival neatly dispatched a tricky question about the partition of the British Raj. "Wow," I said finally, with typical eloquence. "That sucks."

"Dude," my friend replied urgently, "you don't even know. It was crazy at school today. People were, like, collapsing in the hallways. The counseling center set up a special grief session, and we all had to go this emergency assembly about suicide prevention. I haven't seen people this upset since that deaf kid from shop class accidentally hung himself while he was masturbating."

"Yeah," I said. "That sucked, too."

At school Monday morning, a girl sat wracked with sobs in front of my homeroom, cradling her backpack like an infant's corpse. "The only one who could understand me is gone," she wailed. A cascade of snot streamed from her nose into her open mouth, where it clung queasily to her tongue like a streak of untrimmed fat on a raw slab of meat. My classes were thickly peppered with dour boys in grimy Nirvana concert T-shirts. Sam informed me that in honor of the fallen, they had vowed to not remove them, or wash them, or wash themselves.

"Until when?" I said, alarmed. "Until he comes back to life?"

"Until they're ready," she said snappishly. "Until they've gotten to the acceptance stage of grief. You're still in denial."

"You're right," I said. Nearby, a boy named Randy Shoemaker, his oversize *In Utero* tee resplendent with streaks of unidentifiable filth, kicked a locker repeatedly, the heavy steel toe of his worn Doc Marten meeting the cheap metal door with a sickening crunch. He managed at least ten kicks before one of the sad-eyed ex-Marines the public school system had hired to police our hallways spirited him roughly away. "I can't believe this is happening."

By lunchtime, it appeared that others had progressed directly to the anger stage. Their rage, however, was directed not at the traditional targets—God, drugs, the deceased—but toward someone else entirely.

"That fucking *cunt*." Leslie Vorderman, a straw-haired girl with the face of a furious pumpkin, had taken the dull metal point of her geometry compass and carved the word KURT into her forearm, tracing the letters over and over again until they were etched indelibly into her flesh. I imagined it had been painful; the K in particular looked angry, throbbing and red, a fine crust of pus beginning to form at the indentation. "She fucking killed him, the fucking whore."

"Who?" I mouthed nervously.

"Courtney." Sarah Carpenter spat out the name, along with several gummy bits of government-issued pasta salad, peppering the front of her flannel shirt. "She killed him, same as if she pulled the trigger herself."

Sarah Koslowski shrieked, "She tricked him into marrying her because she's the spawn of Satan, and she got him hooked on drugs, and now he's dead. I bet he didn't even do it. I'll bet you a million, trillion dollars she fucking had him killed."

Leslie Vorderman wrenched a fresh scab from the wound on her arm, wincing as she dabbed at the newly bubbling blood with a corner of her dingy paper napkin.

"Don't do that!" I cried. "It'll scar."

"That's the fucking point," she hissed malevolently. "I

want a fucking scar. I want it so that if I run into that bitch someday, I can shove it in front of her ugly fat crack whore face. She deserves to die." The bloody napkin fluttered to the ground, where it came to rest atop a forgotten sandwich, the bread blackened and misshapen where someone had trodden on it in the rush to the door.

Four months ago, I would not have been sitting at this lunch table. But four months ago, I had been unceremoniously evicted from my tenuous position in the outer orbit of the preppy, "popular" clique, when my former "best friend," glimpsing a strategic opportunity for advancement, "accidentally" revealed my crush on the on-again off-again boyfriend of the school's Queen Bee. The depths of my feelings toward him, while embarrassing, were not in and of themselves grounds for expulsion—after all, half the school felt the same way. But unforgivable was the growing communal suspicion that he liked me, too—a belief predicated on the slim but undeniable evidence that he had called me three times on the phone (twice for homework assignments, once just to talk), had kindly made sure I was invited to several parties and after-school hangout sessions from which I otherwise would almost certainly have been excluded, and had told several people he thought I was pretty and that he would certainly be interested in seeing my boobs, should I wish to reveal them. Although I never attempted to act on this or any other invitation, I was swiftly (and publicly) put in my place. On the day of my formal excommunication, I hid for more than four hours in one of the crumbling stalls of the girls bathroom in the basement, shaking with grief and horror at my friend's betrayal and figuring I would have to change schools.

"It's not that I hate you," my ex-friend had smirked, when I tearfully asked her what I had done to make her turn on me like this. "But it's your own fault. You're the one who walks around in those tight shirts, smiling at him all the time. I had to let everyone know what a slut you are."

"I'm not a slut."

"No," she had said thoughtfully, "but you would be if you could be. I had to tell. Otherwise, I would have been a bad friend."

I never heard it suggested even in the subtlest way that the boy might be at fault. He went about his business, his friends, his basketball games with his place in the hierarchy intact. He never spoke to me again.

Luckily, it was almost Christmas, and during the break I was able to pull myself together and consider my options. As the Mean Girls had always given me the rationale that I had been left out of the inner circle because I was "too weird," I threw myself on the mercy of quite a different crowd of girls, who held sullen court on the lawn before and after school, inexpertly smoking cigarettes and scribbling sorrowful slogans on the rubber edges of their Chuck Taylor One Stars. After all, I reasoned, at least we liked the same music. Despite the fuchsia streaks in my hair and a revised wardrobe newly acquired from Goodwill, these girls treated me with palpable hostility at first, like expressionless CIA operatives wearing down a Soviet defector to see where his real loyalties lay. I was endlessly, mercilessly questioned: Were the new streaks in my hair Kool-Aid or Manic Panic? What brand of cigarettes did I prefer, and how many could I smoke without throwing up? Most important, what had brought about this change? Had I actually come to see the inherent pointlessness of life, or was it just that the prepster conformists wouldn't have me anymore?

I answered, "It was when the prepster conformists wouldn't have me anymore that I realized the inherent pointlessness of life." With some surprise, I realized this was perfectly true. Some bullshit has a strange kind of power. I was in.

My new girlfriends didn't seem to enjoy my company much

more than my old ones had, but I felt more secure with them. The petty undermining and backbiting—the ritual disclosure of secrets, the constant jockeying for position—that had so plagued my former life was kept to a minimum here. But now, hearing the people I had treated as my haven, my refuge from the pettiness, from the internalized misogyny that had characterized my previous female friendships—this festering, wrongheaded sense that all women were somehow natural enemies—was heartbreaking.

It wasn't that I saw Courtney Love as a role model. Even through the self-pitying opacity of my adolescent angst it was fairly clear to me that she had some pretty serious emotional problems, to say the least. But in the early '90s, emotional problems were de rigueur, and I couldn't help but feel that Courtney had gotten a bit of a raw deal in the public imagination. Yes, she was an opportunist. Yes, she probably had a personality disorder. Yes, she had used heroin while pregnant (allegedly!) But what about the man who (allegedly!) had used heroin right along with her all that time? The tortured, unstable, desperately unhappy man who had now departed the planet, leaving her alone with a baby, a drug problem, and an army of maniacal fans screaming for her blood? Wasn't it his kid, his problem, his *life*, too?

It took a special kind of guts to be a fuckup as a woman, I thought. To say to hell with being a nice girl, the responsible one, the one who makes sure the man takes care of himself and eats properly and doesn't take too many drugs. To be just as nihilistic and self-destructive as a man, knowing all along that you'll get crucified for it, because somehow, the world will make everything your fault. He'll be a martyr, and you'll be a succubus. He'll be a genius, and you'll be a groupie. He'll be a hero, and you'll be an ugly fat crack whore who deserves to die.

"They should just turn her over to us," Sarah Koslowski was saying. "Mob justice."

Randy Shoemaker had appeared from nowhere, the heady ripeness of his body odor mixing with the thick scent of artificial cheese. "I hope she gets raped," he said, with terrifying matter-of-factness.

"Yeah," said his friend, a boy with greasy green hair whose name I didn't know. "Except you can't rape a whore."

The girls tittered.

"Shut up," I said.

Leslie Vorderman's giant head swiveled slowly in my direction. "What?"

"I said, shut up," I said, my voice gaining strength. "That's a disgusting thing to say. She lost her husband. She's a widow, with a baby. This isn't her fault."

"What are you saying?" Leslie's eyes cut through me like a rusty blade.

"That he shouldn't have done it," I said. "I think it's fucked up how everyone is blaming her. The girls are always blamed. He killed *himself*. And I don't care how depressed he was; I don't think that makes him a hero. If he were a hero, he'd still be alive for the people who need him. Including," I waved my hands shyly around the table, in a gesture of goodwill, "us."

Leslie shot to her feet. "You know what I think?" She didn't wait for me to answer before she thrust her wounded forearm in my face. The inflamed letters were less than an inch from my skin; I could smell the acrid metallic tang of fresh blood. "I think you're a fucking poseur."

She and the Sarahs snatched up their orange plastic trays and flounced away. Randy Shoemaker threw a napkin toward me in halfhearted disgust, and he and his green-haired friend, too, were gone.

"That's okay," I said to myself softly. "I can think of worse things to be."

ANITA AND ME

Deborah Siegel

⁓

I was born in 1969—a year when many women in America were just waking up. The year before I was born, radical feminists protested sex-segregated help wanted ads at newspapers around the nation. Organizations like 9-5 were organizing professional women on the job, while the AFL-CIO held its first statewide women's conference to discuss the status of women in unions in Wisconsin—one state over from where I grew up. Women were launching campaigns for free childcare, the ERA was presented to the state legislatures for ratification, and Helen Reddy's "I Am Woman" hit number one on the charts. You get the picture. It was a heady time to be born a girl.

Like other happily oblivious little girls growing up in the suburbs, I was watching *Sesame Street* and eating HoHos in the living room while both parents worked and my mother went back to school. Words like "pay equity" and "sexual discrimination" were distant concepts, language just beginning to ooze

click

into adult consciousness while I was busy being a Brownie, earning badges for learning how to plant a garden and sew.

In 1979, when I was ten years old, a legal scholar named Catharine MacKinnon argued that sexual harassment was a form of sex discrimination under Title VII of the Civil Rights Act. Her argument was adopted by the U.S. Supreme Court my junior year in high school. None of this registered on my radar, however, until the year I graduated from college.

My "click" of emergent feminist consciousness came fast and furious. She had a name: Anita Hill.

I'll never forget that day Anita entered my living room through an endless loop of media feed. It was October 1991, and Clarence Thomas had been nominated to the Supreme Court by then-President George H. W. Bush to replace retiring Justice Thurgood Marshall. Anita Hill, then a law professor at the University of Oklahoma, came forth with allegations of workplace sexual harassment by Thomas back when they had worked together at the Equal Employment Opportunity Commission in the early 1980s. Information from an FBI interview about the allegations was leaked to the media a few days before the final Senate vote on Thomas's appointment. The vote was postponed. Hearings were held. And televised. Live.

Hill gave graphic descriptions of how Thomas had repeatedly asked her out on dates and continuously talked of pornography and lewd sexual acts. (You remember, right? Pubic hairs on Coke cans. Long Dong Silver. Oh boy.) All the while, she sat poised before an all-white-male Senate Judiciary Committee for three long days, her credibility attacked, while Thomas denied it all. "I categorically denied all of the allegations and denied that I ever attempted to date Anita Hill, when first interviewed by the FBI. I strongly reaffirm that denial," he said. It was "he said" versus "she said," and in the end, he won.

Two days after the hearings ended, the Senate voted 52–48 in favor of Thomas's confirmation. Anita Hill went back to teaching—and became the subject of intense scrutiny when Congress passed a resolution to investigate the leak of the FBI interview. Her phone records were subpoenaed and her family members questioned in a months-long investigation.

But it was hardly over.

In addition to galvanizing those predisposed to embrace classic feminist ideas, Anita Hill's ordeal drew in a slew of new believers—including, yes, me. Her battle framed a younger generation's understanding of women, politics, and power. Because of Anita, scads of younger women realized that some of the rights we had taken for granted were tentative at best. Those of us just entering the professional workforce learned that the battle for equality was not as resolved as it seemed. We learned that accused sexual harassers could get promoted to Supreme Court Justice, while the women who accused them got discredited and disgraced. And we also learned that not all women saw feminism the same.

Anita Hill was my inauguration to feminist activism, and she simultaneously inaugurated me to its opposition. For some women, Hill's testimony against Thomas and her subsequent humiliation and vilification turned them off to feminism with a vengeance. Hill was a catalyst, in other words, for a backlash fueled largely, this time, by women themselves.

The opposition was complex, varied, intense. Women who already felt empowered experienced the Hill affair as a setback. Some formed an ad hoc group known as Women for Judge Thomas. Others felt massively disempowered by the spectacle of a woman—a black woman, no less—capturing national attention by speaking out against the second African American Supreme Court nominee. There was no doubt: The symbolism of a black man being charged by a black woman in front of an all-white jury of all-male senators was eerie. That Hill's accusations could make or break this historic appointment was a disgrace, many black women in particular felt, and, more so, to feminism.

click

Some women, unsympathetic to Hill's complaints, felt she was an outspoken "uppity woman" who gave all women trying to make it in a man's world a bad name. Antifeminist fervor ran strong. I remember conversations with liberal (I had thought) relatives who felt that Hill was some kind of embarrassment. Those on the left divided, and race versus gender became all the rage. It was one of the first times I viscerally declared my politics to loved ones who viscerally disagreed.

But whether you were among those proudly sporting an "I Believe Anita" pin on your backpack or lapel, or a member of Women for Judge Thomas, one thing was certain: Anita had an impact. Because of Hill, "sexual harassment" became a household term. Women spoke out en masse about their own experiences of being sexually harassed by male bosses on the job. According to the National Organization for Women, between 1990 and 1995, sexual harassment cases reported to the EEOC rose by 153 percent. Groups with names like African American Women in Defense of Ourselves channeled women's outrage at the hearings into activism. And other organizations with names like the Independent Women's Forum and the Women's Freedom Network sprang up as well, their founders hoping to harness the Hill opposition and counter the swell of post-Hill feminist activity. It was dizzying for someone like me—who suddenly found herself in the eye of the storm.

For during those days that Anita Hill had taken the stand, I had taken a stand, professionally speaking. I had been interviewing for positions as an assistant editor at a number of glossy women's magazines that month, and suddenly, it all felt moot. I ended up taking a job with a nonprofit, an organization called the National Council for Research on Women, and writing a report on what we knew—and what we needed to know— about sexual harassment. I was living in New York City, far from my Midwestern roots, calling up researchers around the country to ask them for their latest thinking on the issue that had suddenly propelled itself to the center of national debate. It was a far cry from the stories I would have been writing at those glossies had I ended up there.

The report—and my boss, who gave me the telephone numbers and set me loose—empowered me, to use an old-fashioned term. My boss believed in my capacity to pull it off in just a few short weeks, and I did. The report was released nationally and sent to every member of Congress. Because of the report, I accompanied the organization's team to the National Conference of Women State Legislators organized by the Center for the American Woman and Politics that year, held at the Hotel del Coronado in San Diego. The keynote speaker was Anita Hill.

The afternoon Hill was slated to speak, a sacred hush fell over the hotel's ballroom. As she entered the room, the crowd unleashed a collective whoop. A number of the women legislators, dressed in boxy suits and heels, took to the tables. Climbing up indignantly while daintily holding onto their skirts, they waved pink cloth napkins wildly in the air and started chanting from the tabletops "We believe Anita!" in a collective voice that made me cry. It makes me cry when I think of it, still.

Before Anita Hill, my budding feminism had been about beauty, in particular, the beauty of discovering women's voices through the relatively safe haven of literature. Books like Toni Morrison's *The Bluest Eye* had proved microawakenings when I read them in college, and I identified strongly with the feminist narrative that coming to voice meant power and redemption for those who had been traditionally, and often multiply, oppressed. "Anger is better—there is a presence in anger," wrote Morrison. With Anita Hill, these lessons became 3D.

At the Hotel del Coronado that afternoon, beauty and anger joined together in the sound of these powerful women legislators cheering Hill on. I added my voice to the choir. It was impossible to resist. Our cheering went on forever, the sound of gratitude for a lone woman's bravery. It was raucous, cathartic, and sheer bliss.

I don't remember what Anita eventually said during her keynote, or how she said it, I was so caught up in the moment. Something historic was happening, and I felt lucky to be a witness. Even the stuffy Victorian architecture of that famous grand hotel seemed to bow to Anita Hill.

That night, I had a dream that stayed with me all the way back to New York. I dreamed that my great-grandfather, the closest my family had to an outright activist, visited me in my sleep. A Russian immigrant and a fierce socialist, he died when I was only six. In the dream, my great-grandfather offered me his silent approval for what I was becoming, or rather, for what I had just become.

When I woke up the next morning, I knew with new certainty what I wanted to be when I grew up. I wanted to be—I *was*—a feminist. What, specifically, that meant, and what it would require of me was yet unresolved; it would take years after Anita Hill took *her* stand for me to figure it out. But thanks to the strength of one woman's voice speaking up and speaking out in response to injustice experienced personally, I joined legions of others in my generation who became politicized. Raised in the shadow of a half-finished women's movement, after Anita, we could never be the same.

◦◦◦

My Number One Must-Have

Amy Spalding

———

Back in 2000, I was in my early twenties, and working as a receptionist at the total epitome of a dead-end job. My office was the kind of place where company executives were perfectly comfortable spouting off racist and sexist remarks. I'd flinch every time our vice president refused to take a call from salespeople and other contacts just because they happened to be black. I tried to ignore being spoken to like a child merely because I was a female in charge of answering the phones. My gut, of course, told me to speak up. My gut knew I shouldn't sit idly by while this stuff went on. My gut said I probably shouldn't work for people who'd condone that kind of behavior. But I'd gotten really good at ignoring my gut.

In my spare time after work, I wasted a lot of hours on the Internet and watched mindless television. I tried to broaden my life with hobbies and interests—though none of them stuck—and I dreamed of going back to college to

click

complete my undergrad degree so I'd be qualified for jobs I didn't hate. A college dropout was not how I'd envisioned myself. I'd graduated high school near the top of my class and had big plans for programs at universities in cities full of possibility. I'd seen my future self as a writer, a theater director, or something else insanely creative.

But those programs, and therefore—as I saw it—those possible futures, took money. And even community college, which I'd resigned myself to and enrolled in, took a focus and dedication I'd found myself lacking, now that my original dreams had been dashed. I couldn't figure out a new path. Instead of summoning strength to forge ahead on a new one or seeking advice to find one, I just stalled. When my coffee shop employer offered me a full-time position that would keep me from attending classes, I accepted. It would just be for a semester, I told everyone, and then I'd be back on track with a new and better plan.

One semester turned into two, and that year turned into five. The coffee shop gave way to jobs at the mall that led eventually to this office job. I gave up on my creative pursuits: I'd stopped writing fiction (I was hardly even *reading* fiction), I'd given up the piano, and I could no longer be found backstage volunteering at local theaters. All of that seemed to belong to the old me, and even when I tried to embrace one of these lost pieces of myself, the memories of time lost and dreams discarded were too heavy with regret and shame. What was lost remained lost.

One night, killing time by going through my usual online routines, I ran across an article on Salon.com about a band called Sleater-Kinney. I must have read the piece five times; by the next day I was still thinking about it. Women rocking out against the sexist culture, the rape, and sexual harassment that went on at Woodstock '99, and how the notion of "girl power" undermined feminism by taking the anger and power of Riot Grrrl and making it pink and glittery and therefore safe for the masses? I hadn't even known I'd been consumed with these subjects, too, but that article awakened multiple wordless emotions that must have been simmering near the surface the whole time.

Since I was a total musical theater nerd whose CD player was usually loaded up with Sondheim, I couldn't imagine that I'd actually like listening to Sleater-Kinney. So I buried my curiosity along with that tumble of emotions the article had generated in me, just like I had nearly ten years ago after reading about Riot Grrrl in *Sassy* magazine. And I guess it could have gone the same way, except that a few weeks later I was flipping channels and landed on MTV2, where this video of three women rocking out played. Their sound was like nothing in my music library for sure, but instead of being turned off I was glued to my screen.

And then the video came to an end, the information went up on the screen, and I learned I'd been watching and listening to Sleater-Kinney. Within five minutes I'd already ordered their latest album, *All Hands on the Bad One*. It arrived just a couple days later.

By now I was actually nervous! This album had been pretty built up, considering I'd somehow gotten obsessed with it and so far had only heard about sixty seconds of one song. Still, I marched right to my CD player, dropped in the disc, and got ready to listen. And I did. And I listened again. I listened a lot that night. I couldn't get enough.

To me on that night, Sleater-Kinney's music resonated for a lot of reasons. Even though my parents had brought me up on 1960s protest folk music, I'd never heard women singing about sexism beyond, you know, Gwen Stefani being "Just a Girl." There was something revolutionary in that, in taking up your own fight, in not being afraid to put it all out there in a time where our culture wasn't exactly clamoring to hear about

177

women's struggles. When I listened to, for example, "#1 Must Have" or "The Professional," my brain was flooded with the same kind of recognition the article had brought on but in a far bigger, more emotional way. It pulsed through my skin.

I felt ideas building inside of me. There was suddenly the possibility that life was limitless, that I was limitless, too. No longer did I define ideas and myself based on what others told me. If these three women could kick down the old guard, why couldn't I?

Of course, there's also the fact that Sleater-Kinney is, besides their feminist ideals, a really kick-ass band. Corin Tucker's wail is like no other; it raised the hairs on the back of my neck with a thrill. I'd never heard anyone, much less a woman only a few years older than myself, make noise like this. Carrie Brownstein on guitar was something otherworldly, too; very few wield the instrument with the skill she possessed. And my quite rhythmless self marveled at Janet Weiss's mastery of the drums. These were *musicians*. And thanks to them, my understanding of what music could be and where it could take you blossomed.

I admit up until that point I'd been one of those girls who thought being a feminist meant casting aside too much concern over my appearance, though maybe that had just been an excuse to be lazy and hide behind shapeless clothes. So when I saw pictures of these women who, in a very short period of time, I'd come to respect in big, huge bunches, I realized I didn't have to keep going through life like I was invisible. In fact, I realized I didn't want to be invisible anymore.

I chopped off my mousy hair, went back to my younger self's habit of dying it bright red. I felt no shame in outfitting my plus-size frame in clothes that made me feel good about myself . . . and actually fit! The ugly, shapeless stuff made for someone twice my age got phased out of my wardrobe. I started putting on makeup every day to maximize my new look. Yeah, it sounds crazy that anyone could show an embrace of feminism by using more beauty products, but for me it wasn't about fitting anyone's ideal of femininity. For me it was about having decided I was worth enough to put, well, literally, a better face forward.

I started making noise, too. Whenever I could get away with it, I pointed out the sexist, racist, classist comments people around me were making. When a coworker defended the actions of a nearby community center for kicking out a theater group just because they were putting on a show featuring gay characters, I politely but loudly let her know she was discriminating and that my attitude of equality had nothing to do with my age or immaturity as she saw it. Quite often I found myself saying, simply, "I don't agree with that," and moving on. I wasn't starting my own revolution, but I was no longer sitting silently. Once my eyes had been opened, I saw more discrimination than I ever realized was out there. I felt armed now though. If I couldn't stop it, I could at least identify it and recognize it for what it was. Before long I walked out of that terrible job with no regrets.

And I started making noise of a different nature, too, when I bought an electric guitar and signed up for lessons. (And I made a lot of noise the day a salesperson at a guitar shop refused to help me compare amps because he assumed I was shopping for my boyfriend and not myself.)

Of course, like a good fan, I purchased the remainder of Sleater-Kinney's catalog. I explored other women who rocked, too, and before long my guitar case was covered with buttons and patches for Le Tigre, the Gossip, Bikini Kill, Bratmobile, Heavens to Betsy, the Bangs, and countless more. I listened to boys who rocked, too. Music had just zipped into my life to fill the little empty gaps, and I'd truly never felt so complete.

Now that everyday life felt so full of joy and possibility, my past seemed a lot less scary. I started seeing those five years as something temporary. I was reading for fun again, and going to movies that excited me on an artistic level. The old me hadn't been truly lost; she'd only stumbled off her path.

And so armed with this new and more fearless sense of worth combined with my old passion coursing through me again, I made lots of phone calls and wrote lots of emails and filled out countless forms. Luckily all of that tedious paperwork paid off, because the next fall I was officially enrolled at the local university that had always been my ideal undergrad school in a communications program where I'd have to be creative constantly. I knew it was still a long road to graduation, but at least I'd started back down it. Plus there is something to be said about the journey; I wasn't wasting any more years wishing for the next thing to happen. Finishing school and moving out of Missouri were definitely on my schedule, but I'd get to them when I was ready. In the meantime I had music and education and writing and a day job I didn't even hate.

It's not that Sleater-Kinney's music—or even feminism, necessarily, though a "This is what a feminist looks like!" button was pinned proudly to my schoolbag—gave all of this to me. What they did was unleash what was already within me, fighting to get out, and shook awake the part of me that thrives on passion and creativity. Sleater-Kinney lent a voice to the trapped one, and she used that to pull herself out.

❧

THE BROWN GIRL'S GUIDE TO LABELS

Mathangi Subramanian

⌐⌐⌐

1998

When they heard that I had been accepted at Brown University, friends from my suburban high school filled my yearbook with dire warnings and heartfelt advice about the cosmetic consequences of my potential liberalization.

"Don't forget to shave your armpits," was a popular one.

"Don't let me see you burning your bra on CNN next year," was another.

When I got to Brown, I was told that getting a degree was important, but that the real reason we were in college was to find ourselves.

I soon discovered that the most common way to find oneself was to adopt a label. Among my white girlfriends, the most popular of these labels was *feminist*.

click

"I'm not saying that men and women shouldn't be different," they told me. "I'm just saying they should be equal."

This sounded about right to me, so I decided to investigate. In between my highly practical science classes, I listened in on spirited conversations about the need to move away from the image of bra-burning, pierced harridans with hairy armpits (this sounded familiar) and toward embracing and celebrating our desire to wear lipstick and short skirts without judgment. Other than a modicum of knowledge I had gained in seventh grade, which is the year I spent wearing foundation and designer skirts in a desperate attempt to cover up my acne and naiveté, I didn't know much about fashion. Then there was the whole battle to reclaim the word *sexy*, a battle I couldn't join simply because I couldn't bring myself to invest in reclaiming a word I had never claimed in the first place, and probably never would. White girls were sexy. Bespectacled Indian girls who took AP physics and ran for president of the debate team were not.

Of course, the whole Indian thing presented another option: Released from the white-washed suburbs, I discovered a contingent of South Asian Americans who embraced their ethnic identities by labeling themselves either as *desi* or *brown*. I occasionally ate lunch with them before lab or spent late nights with them working on problem sets. The girls ironed their hair, wore huge earrings, and lusted after South Asian boys who shortened their names to "Jay" or "Ace" and wore too much cologne.

"Oh my god, did you hear Deepti likes Jay?" went a typical conversation.

"Seriously. You know she's just trying to snag a husband," it continued.

"Um, gross. Wait, I totally saw the perfect wedding sari online yesterday, wanna see?" it usually ended.

Well, clearly this wasn't going to work. It wasn't until years later that I discovered that these girls were the minority, and that there was a whole subset of desi women who fantasized about political activism and artistic fame, rather than elaborate weddings. At the time, though, I thought that brown was not the label for me.

By the end of my freshman year, I had picked out several potential majors, and no potential labels.

1999

The summer I turned nineteen, I went to India for the second time in my life and hated every minute. I spent half the time sitting silently on display before a parade of relatives who discussed me in Tamil as if I weren't there. The other half I spent cursing my weak stomach: If I wasn't throwing up, I was popping Pepto Bismol.

One morning, while I was sitting on the balcony attempting to catch the weak excuse for a breeze, my mother came out and patted my sweaty hair.

"How you doing?" she asked, flopping into a chair next to me.

"Ugh," I said, wiping the sweat pooled around my temples.

My mother's mother wandered out onto the balcony, wiping her brow with her sari. My *patthi* is impossibly intelligent, able to rattle off everything from the symptoms associated with rare diseases to the color of the heroine's sari in every Tamil movie ever made. In later years, when I visited, we would watch Tamil serials together, and she would provide a running commentary that confirmed my theory that facility with sarcasm is a genetic trait. That summer, though, we did not yet know how much we had in common. To me, she was still a quirky, vacant woman prone to non sequiturs.

"Mathangi, when are you getting married?" she asked me in Tamil.

"Amma!" my mom yelled. "She's only nineteen. Leave her alone."

click

"She should start thinking now," my grandmother said. "She must get married before she's too old."

"She doesn't have to get married at all," my mom said, stroking my hair, but staring defiantly at my grandmother. "I've always told her and her brother that they should be independent. There's no reason for her to get married if she's not in love."

"Not for love," my grandmother said, unexpectedly switching into her choppy Indian English. "Just to have someone to take care of you."

"She can take care of herself," my mother said firmly, her hands raking through my hair with increasingly violent strokes.

I wandered inside and found my brother huddled beneath the ceiling fan, reading the paper.

"What are you doing?" I asked him.

"Finding you a husband," he said without looking up.

"Seriously?" I said.

"Yeah," he said, pushing his glasses up on his nose. "But you're doomed." He said *doomed* the way my family always said that word to each other: with a thick Indian accent, rolling our tongues around the d's. "Basically, they all want someone to cook them curry."

"What?" I said. "I make damn good curry."

"It's not about how good the curry is," he said. "It's about focusing your skill set. As in, only being able to make curry. In this market, autonomy and independent thought seem to be discouraged. But hey, if you drop out of college, you might still make the cut. If you finish, you'll be overqualified."

My grandmother slid up beside me and placed her gnarled hand on my shoulder. Her wrinkled brown skin always reminded me of walnuts.

"Mathangi," she said, "men are useless. Your mother is right. Don't get married."

"Oh," I said. "Okay. Um, thanks."

184

"Good," she said. She nodded, adjusted the *pallu* of her sari, and walked resolutely into the kitchen.

My brother tapped the paper excitedly. "Hey, this guy wants someone with a master's degree. I bet he'd settle for someone with a bachelor's," he said. "This is it! This is your man!"

"Be still my beating heart," I said.

2002

After I graduated from college, I prepared to move to the border of Mexico, where I had landed my first job: teaching chemistry at a public high school. My family was pleased, but my girlfriends were not.

"But don't you want to go to India?" they asked. "I mean, women there are *so* oppressed. Don't you want to help people where you're from?"

I didn't want to go to India and suffer through a year or two of mosquito bites the size of quarters and frequent trips to pit toilets in the middle of nowhere. I wanted to live in the United States and eat whatever I chose and sleep without a mosquito net and cross the street without fear of death-by-autorickshaw. And if it came down to where I was from, I was from America. American girls were failing out of school and living in poverty and raising babies when they were still in their teens. It seemed like I could really make a difference here, at home.

Besides, I wasn't sure what feminism had to do with it. It's not like any Indian women I knew wore makeup, other than a little bit of eyeliner now and then, and why wear a short skirt when you could wear a sari?

2003

"*Mmmff*, hello?"

"Honey? Did I wake you?"

I forced myself to sit up, blinking in the South Texas sunlight that seeped through the slats of the blinds on my windows.

"Mom, is that you?" I asked, fumbling for my glasses. "What time is it?"

"It's eight o'clock," she said. "Do you want me to call back? Were you sleeping in?"

"No, no," I said, yawning. "Is everything okay?"

"I have big news," she said. I could hear the rhythm of a knife on a cutting board in the background, and I knew that, as she often did, she was cooking as she spoke to me.

"Oh?" I said, getting out of bed and padding across the carpet into my own kitchen, fully stocked with small Tupperware containers of spices my mother gave me when I left home.

"I told you I read that book you gave me, the book about men and makeup?" she said.

"*The Beauty Myth*," I said. She had stopped buying makeup after she read it.

"Yes, that one! Well, I just read that other book you got me. *Sex and Power?*"

"Right," I said. I hadn't read it at the time, but my mom had just gotten a hard won promotion, so I thought it was appropriate.

"I related to every single page!" she said. "It was like reading my life. There were all these stories about women taking care of their family and working full-time, and how they can't put in the same hours as men because they have to go home and cook dinner, which, you know, I used to do." My mom had taught my father to cook when she went back to school for her associate's degree in computer science and couldn't work, study, and run the house by herself anymore. "And then there was a whole part about how women get passed over for promotions," she continued. What she didn't mention is that, when she figured out her boss had passed her over the last time for yet another white male, she had marched into his office and declared loudly with the door open, "I can be a lot of things, but I can't be white!" *She* got the promotion two weeks later.

"So then I realized something," she said. I could hear the crackle of mustard seeds in hot oil, and my stomach began to rumble.

"Tell me," I said, pushing aside a stack of my students' ungraded chemistry tests to make room on the counter for a box of cereal.

"I'm a feminist!" she said, exhaling all at once.

"Wow, Mom, that's great," I said, weakly.

"Isn't that wonderful? I have been all this time, and we just didn't have a word for it," she said. I heard a splatter and she said, "Oh, hold on, I'm just adding some potatoes to the oil. Just a second."

As I chewed on my cereal, I wondered how everyone in the world seemed to be okay with the label feminist when I wasn't. Lately, I had been working my way through the collection of books about India in the local public library, particularly the ones about Indian women, which I noticed seemed to be mostly written by non-Indian women. If these books were to be believed then Indian women were submissive, abused, mouselike creatures draped in bright colors and regrets. No matter where I looked, the message was clear: You could be Indian, and you could be a feminist, but you couldn't be both.

And yet, here was my mother, who grew up in a village in the South of India, declaring herself a feminist. If she was a feminist, was I?

2006

During my second semester of graduate school, it was time, yet again, to pick a label.

click

"Don't forget that one of the key parts of writing the methodology section of any ethnography is to discuss your positionality," my professor said. "You should also describe what kind of researcher you are. You might be postmodern for example, or a positivist, or a feminist."

Groan, that word again.

"I'm passing out a couple of articles that may help you decide what you are," she said, passing out a thick packet of reading.

I began reading the packet on the subway the next day. I flipped through the essays and scanned the titles and the authors' names. Then, suddenly, I stopped.

"Chandra Mohanty?" I said out loud, feeling the familiar taste of an Indian name on my tongue. I began to read. And read. And read. And I missed my stop and ended up in Brooklyn. I got out of the train, crossed the platform, and began to read again.

Mohanty called herself a third world feminist. She talked about how Western feminists fought for the right to work, while third world feminists acknowledged that women did most of the world's work, and were therefore fighting for the right to rest. She talked about how third world women fought their battles in the home, defying their family's rules about gender roles. She celebrated daily acts of defiance, like rejecting the necessity of marriage or insisting that men contribute to household chores, and said they required just as much sacrifice and courage as attending any rally in the streets. The stories she told were those of my aunts and my mother and my grandmothers, and, of course, myself.

Now this feminism fit. I wrapped it around me and snuggled in it, the yards of words like the soft fabric of my grandmother's saris.

2008

One morning, before the SAT class I started teaching at a community center in Queens, one of my Indian American students came to class with delicate swirls of henna all over her hands.

"What's with the *mendhi?*" I asked her. "Did someone get married?"

"It's Karwa Chauth," she said, holding out her hands so I could admire them. "Wives are supposed to fast for their husband's health. Are you fasting, miss?"

"No," I said, touching the tips of her fingers approvingly. "I don't have a husband, and I hate fasting. Did your mom do it?"

"Yes," she said. "And so do I."

"Who do you fast for?" I asked.

"My husband," she said. Then, seeing the look on my face, she added, "I mean, my future husband."

"Why?" I asked. "You have plenty of time to worry about being married! Worry about your career and your education now, not your marriage. Besides, it's not like your future husband is fasting for you."

"Actually," she said, "my boyfriend did fast for me."

"Really?" I asked. "Is that common?"

"Well, no," she said. "And especially not him. He's Bangladeshi and Muslim. But I told him I was doing it, and so we agreed that it was only fair if he did it, too. So he is."

"Wow," I said, truly impressed. I was about to tell her that she was quite the young feminist, but I stopped myself. I had dropped the word on the center before, and the girls usually rolled their eyes and told me, "That word's for white ladies."

How could I correct them? Two years before, I had agreed with them. I suppose I could've explained how after reading Chandra Mohanty, I had discovered Uma Narayan and Kumari Jayawardena. I could describe how I had read essay after essay about families and religion and food and history, and how I had discovered a strand of feminism that resonated with me

189

and didn't require me to compromise myself or my past or my future. I could share my realization that every Indian woman I have ever met is a feminist, and every Bangladeshi and Sri Lankan and Pakistani woman, too, because the only place I have ever met submissive desi women is between the pages of books written by women who do not live in our community.

But what was the point? Labeled or unlabeled, brown women everywhere are struggling for each other. No matter what people call them—or, I should say, no matter what people call us—what matters the most is what we call ourselves.

WORD AND DEED

J. Courtney Sullivan

One of the sounds I associate most with my childhood is the *click-clicking* of high heels on the front walk sometime after dusk each night. Through the window, I'd hear my mother coming home from work and feel a little jolt of excitement. When the door opened, she'd often be laden down with grocery bags, and the smell of her perfume—it was called Creation—filled the hallway.

She worked in television and later had her own public relations firm. She won two Emmy awards before she turned thirty. Some years, she outearned my father, a lawyer who worked from home when both I and my sister (who is younger by almost a decade) were small. In some ways, he has always been the more stereotypically feminine of the pair. He is sweet and sensitive and gentle. When they got engaged, my mother told him she didn't do laundry. To this day, all dirty clothes at 32 Garden Street are the province of my dad.

click

As a little girl, I went to the office with my mother from
time to time. She set me up at a desk, where I worked on various imaginary projects and treated her indulgent assistant as my
own. But for the most part, my mother's professional self was a
mystery to me. The clothes she wore to work—dark skirt suits
and silk scarves and three-inch, pointy-toed heels—were like a
uniform for that other part of her, the part that existed offstage.
They suggested something bigger and better and more exciting
than our 1980s suburban existence had to offer. After bedtime, while my parents watched the news downstairs, I would
occasionally snoop about in their room, sneaking one of my
mother's scarves out of her closet and wrapping it around my
hair, Marilyn Monroe style. I'd breathe in the scent of Creation
and imagine who I might become.

I liked boys a lot, but unlike many of my friends, I never
planned a wedding. When we played house, I was always the
mom—the working mom who walked in the door at seven
and kicked off her stilettos before starting dinner. I thought
a lot about my career. I wanted to be a writer, an actress, a
hairstylist, a lawyer, and a fashion designer. I saw no reason
why I couldn't be all five at once. Instead of stickers, I col-
lected While You Were Out notepads, on which my imaginary
secretary Denise left me dozens of urgent messages. At eight,
I got in trouble for opening up the yellow pages and ordering
furniture for my office—real desks, chairs, lamps, and tables, for
the make-believe employees of my fashion line, CoCo Designs.
(Not a terribly original name, but I suppose if you're going to
steal, you might as well steal from Chanel.)

Without discussing it in any sort of academic way—without
discussing it at all, really—my parents taught me through their
actions about the possibilities of gender balance in a marriage.
They taught me that a woman can be powerful and opinionated and strong-willed, and at the same time be maternal
and warm; that a man can be simultaneously masculine and

nurturing, and he might just know things about fabric softener that his wife could never guess.

Mostly because of what I saw in other people's homes, I knew that our life was atypical for both our town and our traditional extended Irish Catholic family. Sometimes, playing at a friend's house, I'd hear her mother threaten, "Wait until your father gets home." In my house, there was no such threat. My mother could be silly and fun and tender and wildly generous, but if she got mad, look out. Another common remark from kids around the neighborhood: "We get to have pizza tonight. Our dad is baby-sitting." I thought this was strange, even then. How can your *parent* be baby-sitting you? In my family, Dad was just as likely as Mom to stay home with you if you were sick, or bring your lunch to school if you forgot it on the kitchen counter.

This is not to say that we lived a life of egalitarian bliss or that I ever gazed out over my Tyson chicken nuggets and complimented my mother on being a perfect model of modern womanhood. I was fiercely proud of her, and in my precocious way, I might remark to a schoolmate, "Oh, your mom's a teacher? Well that's nice, but mine's VP of communications." Even so, I was often jealous of the fact that other kids in my neighborhood didn't come home to baby-sitters after school, or have to go to day camp in the summertime. Their stay-at-home moms effortlessly made French braids and brownies or decorated sweatshirts with iron-on Easter bunny appliqués and puffy paint. They took wreath-making classes and hung seasonal flags from poles on their front porches. My mother didn't have time for all that. Our Christmas lights were usually still up in March. If I begged her for a puffy paint sweatshirt, she'd make me one. But her letters were off, the iron-on slightly lumpy. I'd let her know that her handiwork wasn't up to snuff by cruelly choosing to wear the perfect shirt my friend Caitlain's mother had made me instead.

click

In middle school, the word *feminism* was just beginning to make its way into my consciousness. Like a lot of women from her generation (and mine), even though my mother embodied what it meant to be a feminist, she never called herself one. If anything, she grew embarrassed and self-conscious when I tried to engage her in a conversation about what it meant to be an independent, professionally successful woman like her—as if I were really just criticizing her for being lousy on the home front. She came from a no-frills, working-class family. She was the first one of them to go to college. She seemed to think there was something negative or self-indulgent about calling oneself a feminist. She once told me, only half-joking, that the women's movement might be just a ploy to get females to do more work, both at the office and around the house. Maybe that's when I began to realize that despite the pretty silk scarves and exciting work stories, my mother was overwhelmed. She seemed to suspect that feminism, if it applied to her at all, was part of what had gotten her into this jam in the first place.

As it is with many girls, my relationship with my mother quickly went from idolizing her as a kid to misunderstanding and disliking her as an adolescent (and right back around to idolizing her as an adult, but we'll get to that later). I had a high school English teacher named Maxine, a writer who understood the importance—and also the limitations—of words. She seemed different from my mother in most every way. I adored her at once. Maxine had long, tanned limbs and dark hair with flecks of gray mixed in. She always wore pants and sensible flats. She drank a lot of coffee. She had no children but owned a beloved standard poodle named Lola, who sometimes slept under the table while our class read Shakespeare aloud. My freshman year, she married a lovely artist in a wedding ceremony officiated by Howard Zinn. And most important of all, she was a loud and proud, card-carrying feminist.

Maxine was the rare sort of teacher who I just wanted to be around all the time. Who, more to the point, I just wanted to *be*. I spent many after-school hours sitting at her desk talking about literature and life and love. Feminism always made its way into the conversation, and she spoke the language with passion. When I began to feel ashamed about my increasingly curvy body, she handed me a copy of *The Beauty Myth*. When I told her about a boy, a former friend who had begun to follow me and make threatening middle-of-the-night phone calls to my house, she explained that some men will systematically implement fear in women, and that we have to be vigilant about it. I did my homework. I began volunteering in a domestic violence shelter. Rather than feel embarrassed or somehow responsible when the guy in question lingered by my locker, I reminded myself that I wasn't alone in it and tried to stand up to him as best I could.

By junior year, my bedroom door was plastered with bumper stickers that said IN GODDESS WE TRUST and FEMINISM IS THE RADICAL NOTION THAT WOMEN ARE PEOPLE. My bookshelves were crammed full of Susan Faludi and Catharine MacKinnon and Andrea Dworkin. I attended rallies and lectures and attempted to engage my uncles in debates about abortion while they were trying to watch Notre Dame football on the couch. I decided to attend a women's college known for its fierce feminist underpinnings. My parents mostly seemed amused by all of this, viewing it as a by-product of teenage-hood, something rough and overly intense that would be tamed in time, like the blue streaks in my hair, or the oxblood Fluevog boots I wore, even in August.

"You're a feminist," I would tell my mother over and over again.

"No I'm not," she'd say.

"Well, why not? What do you think it *means*, anyway?"

"Oh please, not this again."

There were moments during these arguments when I won-

click

dered why I was pushing so hard, why it even mattered for my mother, for anyone, to take on the label, especially when she was clearly *practicing* feminism every day. But Maxine had taught me that naming is crucial, because it gives you the strength to realize that you're part of something larger than just you, and that knowledge provides both the comfort of belonging to a community and the rage to fight back. Being a feminist, I found, was like being part of an extended family. Sure, there was some infighting and some crazy gossip, some misunderstanding and intergenerational befuddlement, but at their best, my fellow feminists—the ones I was beginning to know personally, and the ones I only knew through books—helped me understand myself in the larger context of our society. They helped me realize I wasn't alone.

I wanted the same thing for my mother, because I believed that if she could see our life through the lens of feminism as I did, she might feel angry, rather than defeated, about the fact that a six-figure salary that supported her kids had always meant bubkes to us compared to an Easter bunny appliqué. Or that she eventually briefly took a job far below her skill and experience level, out of a sense of guilt that made her think she ought to work fewer hours, and in our hometown. Or that though she never intended to change her name, people always called her "Mrs. Sullivan" anyway. Or that she was sometimes stigmatized by other mothers for working, while my father was considered a lesser God for helping around the house by the divorced moms of some of my friends. ("He plays hair salon with you, puts you to bed, *and* does the dishes?")

I began to see that the members of our family—my mother most of all—were victims of a culture that devalues caretaking in the home while at the same time fetishizing it, making domesticity synonymous with love and the ability to control; allowing women to make inroads professionally, but punishing them if they cannot, as they say, have it all. (By which, they, of course, mean do it all.) Those other mothers in my neighborhood, with their brownies and their wreath-making and their long dull days in the house, were no doubt victims of this, too. That same (please allow me to use the p-word here) patriarchal culture benefited every time a razor-sharp, ambitious, incredible woman like my mother decided she wasn't a feminist, because that decision left her isolated and disenfranchised, instead of empowered, connected, and pissed off.

As I went through college and the years that followed, I stopped trying to recruit my mother to feminism in a direct, aggressive way. (The blue hair and the Fluevogs vanished, too.) But I often wrote about it and continued to wonder whether she might one day change her mind. I'd recommend books by feminist authors, invite her to lectures, and detail long conversations I'd had with like-minded friends, in the hopes that she might come around. My sister jumped on the bandwagon with me, and so there were two of us in the house preaching the Gospel According to Steinem. But for years, I never asked my mother directly anymore, perhaps because I was afraid of her answer.

Last week, as I sat down to write this, I thought *What the hell* and emailed my mom and asked, *Would you call yourself a feminist?* She responded right away: *Yes I would. Don't forget to send Grandma a birthday card.* Rarely have I felt such joy just from reading the words on a computer screen.

In both word and deed, feminism is something we only really understand after we've been exposed to it, after someone else has taught us what it looks like and how it can help make our lives all the richer. Maxine gave me the language of feminism, and that set me on a path to becoming the woman I am today. But it was my mother—with her passion for her career and her family, her unwillingness to conform to what someone else deemed feminine—who gave me the tools. I'd like to think she made me a feminist in her way, and that I made her one in mine.

∽◎∾

ON READING KATIE ROIPHE

Rebecca Traister

⌐

I was born a feminist, or at the very least delivered tidily into a feminist family. My parents were liberals, academics, who had marched on Washington for civil rights, and who believed in professional and economic equality for everyone, "regardless of race, creed, gender, or place of national origin"—one of the first phrases my dad taught me to say.

Though my mother hadn't done much marching on behalf of the feminist movement, she had lived it. One of the first two women hired in her English department; one of the first to have children; one of the first to be granted tenure. Her sister, my aunt, had been more vocal and active in the women's movement and was a feminist scholar.

In most every family I knew as a child, mothers made as much or more money than fathers. I wasn't allowed Barbies as a girl (though I pined for them) and I was not encouraged to play princess (not a problem). One of my first friends, as a toddler, was a girl who dressed in Wonder Woman Under-roos and Osh-Kosh overalls; she grew up to be the slam poet Alix Olsen. Her mom was a feminist, too.

Somewhere in the back of the closet in my childhood bedroom is a Mondale-Ferraro button, a reminder of the 1984 election in which my father brought me into the voting booth so that, at nine, I might cast my first-ever vote for the first-ever woman on a major-party presidential ticket.

And on a bookshelf somewhere near that jewelry box is the roughed-up paperback of *The Handmaid's Tale*, Margaret Atwood's novel of a dystopian future in which women are enslaved baby-incubators who have been stripped of identity. I picked that one up at thirteen, on a vacation with my family, powering through it in three days, to the consternation of my mother and my aunt, who tried unsuccessfully to muffle their concerns that it would scare the bejesus out of me. It didn't. The book captivated me, but I did not understand it enough to be frightened.

At sixteen, I proudly hung a yellow sash on my bedroom door, not from any beauty contest or prom contest or equestrian event, but from the 1992 march on Washington for reproductive rights. I remember boarding the buses with a high school friend and her mother, traveling to DC with our brown-bagged lunches, and spending the day floating around the Mall gawking at the little knots of like-minded but different-looking women and men. When I looked at the aerial photos of the march the next day in the paper, I could hardly believe that I had been a dot in that sea of people.

I had it all: the signifiers, the talking points. I knew what coat hangers represented, had, well . . . skimmed *The Feminine Mystique*. I'd read *Our Bodies, Ourselves* and could unwillingly acknowledge to an inquisitive teacher that my devotion to *Pretty Woman* was problematic from some gender-inflected standpoints.

It's tempting to think that I was simply popped out into a world that taught me to care enough about gender politics to make it a part of my daily adult life. But I just don't think it was that easy. For six years now, I have made my living writing about women and power and media and politics, and I just don't think it's because I went to that march in 1992.

While those early brushes with good old-fashioned feminism certainly marked and shaped me, none of them pulled me headlong into the fray. Reading grown-up novels about dark sexual politics, importantly pulling a voting booth curtain closed behind me and my dad, marching in the nation's capitol: They were all versions of dressing up in my mother's clothes, tottering around in her shoes. They were exercises in inherited politics and performed adulthood—useful, invaluable, perhaps, to the development of my own ideology, but not born of my own experience.

No, the moment I got propelled—rather nauseatingly, if I remember correctly—into a feminism that would continue to engage me in a mental tussle over the circumstances, rights, futures, and power dynamics of gender took place in the fall of 1993, during my freshman year of college, in a shared bedroom in the Delta Delta Delta fraternity house.

It was there—not in the midst of a romantic or sexual assignation, but on a run for more clear grain alcohol to pour into the trash can serving as a punch bowl downstairs—that I first spied, on the floor next to a mussed bed, a black-and-white hardcover book, its title slashed in crimson: *The Morning After: Sex, Fear, and Feminism on Campus.*

The book was by Katie Roiphe, a young English doctoral candidate at Princeton, the daughter of a second-wave feminist writer, Anne Roiphe. It had been published, with much fanfare, including a provocative excerpt in *The New York Times Magazine*, in June of my senior year of high school. It posited that the feminist movement had left college women with a

click

bad Take Back the Night–juiced habit of crying wolf about date rape, claiming victimhood—a state that Roiphe positively abhorred—when in fact they should have been taking responsibility: for drinking, for dressing provocatively, for engaging in what Roiphe called "bad sex," and then for waking up the next morning and calling it date rape.

I had seen the book and been aware of the coverage of it in the summer before my freshman year. But having not then been to college, not yet experienced the keg-standing Greek life, having never felt the push of an unwanted or insistent hand or mouth, having never seen my female friends straggle home in the early hours of the morning, only to curl up in their beds to cry and sleep through the next day, it hadn't made much of an impact on me.

But just a few months into college, my worldview shifted. And seeing that book, sitting in that fraternity bedroom on a night that might well end with some other hall mate coming home in tears, hit me in the solar plexus. I'd already had several friends who had experienced sexual encounters that they did not officially refer to as rape, but that had certainly been more unwanted, more unsolicited, more scarring, and more terrible than what Roiphe so confidently wrote off—from her perch at Princeton, far across the country, far across from the campus life I now recognized—as a fun night gone slightly awry.

Of course, I realized even then, the volume in the fraternity bedroom was likely there because the student who occupied the room had been assigned it in a sociology or psychology or American studies or women's studies class, not because he was some junior Roiphe acolyte. But that didn't matter to me that night, when I felt a roiling discomfort, as a realization dawned: Conversations about women and power didn't just take place in Washington or in *The New York Times* or in voting booths. They were happening all around; they were about how my peers and I were living our daily lives; they might even have an impact on how we felt about ourselves, how we evaluated our choices and judged ourselves, and how other people evaluated our behaviors, dress, and attitudes.

Later in my freshman year, *The Morning After* was assigned to me in a big survey class about human sexuality. On the day the professor, a feminist, gave her critical lecture about it, I watched as several pairs of young men around the auditorium snickered and gave each other not-so-subtle high-fives beneath the fold-out writing desks.

And the first time was not the last time that I would see the book in a fraternity house, where, in that freshman year, it became a winking talisman of a new, Roiphe-fortified immunity against the specter of the imagined date-rape accuser. To my knowledge, not one student in my freshman class ever filed rape charges, though the stream of young women with crumpled faces, ripped clothing, or occasional black-and-blue marks continued to drip through the hallways, back to their beds.

I suppose that this would be a better tale if I had exhibited a dramatic response to Roiphe's book: if I had marched out of a class, or raged and burned the volume in effigy, if I had led Take Back the Night rallies or made donations to feminist organizations in Roiphe's name. But that was not my reaction. In truth, I was never much of a Take Back the Night girl myself, I didn't have money to make donations, and I rarely made public proclamations. (Though in a moment of high dudgeon a few years later, I refused to shake Roiphe's hand when she arrived for a meeting at an office where I worked.)

No, mostly what Roiphe made me do as an eighteen-year-old was consider, quietly and hard, the fact that feminism was not just my mother's, or Roiphe's mother's for that matter. It was not just about coat hangers and reproductive rights or who was on a presidential ticket, though of course it was about those things, too. Roiphe showed me that thinking and arguing about feminism ran through my every day, through the every day of my friends. That feminism matters to the way a woman is looked at when she orders a beer, when she wears a certain skirt, when she raises her hand in class, when she gets on the cover of *The New York Times Magazine* for bagging on other women. Roiphe showed me what my mother's feminism could not: that there were still messy battles to be fought.

Of course, at the time, I didn't think about it exactly that way. What I thought about, for silent hours, sometimes, was how much I loathed this unknown person named Katie Roiphe. I thought about how bad she made girls feel; I thought about the transparency of her desire to speak directly to the men who would gladly take her permission to continue to treat women as provocative flirts who owed them sex. I thought about the fact that she had gotten famous (in a collegiate context, at least) for selling out women, for making them hate themselves more than they already did, for making them punish themselves for having felt pain or fear to begin with.

Now, it's almost difficult to remember what precisely about *The Morning After* got me quite so hot. In years since, I've encountered so much more backlash rhetoric that Roiphe's seems a tame blip in comparison. As an adult—who has since met and profiled Roiphe, and disclosed my youthful dismay to her and to readers—I have come to value her at the very least as a reliably ballsy feminist irritant, and at the very most as a talented writer and a beloved teacher of young journalists who enables important conversations by continuing to infuriate me and many of my peers. I still disagree heartily with most of what she writes, but I no longer hate her for writing it.

Part of me also wishes that she hadn't been the one to make feminism live and breathe for me. Back then, though I didn't realize it, it was a terrible cliché to revile Roiphe. Her mission (and reward) was to ruffle feathers, and the fact that she so successfully ruffled mine leaves me more than a little chagrined. I also wish that it hadn't been animus toward another woman that so deeply engaged me. Oh, to fall into the clichés we most deplore!

For many women out there, those who were not steeped in the attitudes of the women's movement from birth, a call to arms surely came from some purer and less fraught source. But alas, for me, it took the aggressive perspective of someone who had been raised as I had but somehow came out differently, to realize that I still had a lifetime of fighting ahead of me.

~∽⊚∾

An Engineering Approach
to Feminism

Janet Tsai

⁓

"**Go** stand next to your sister," a ten-year-old boy on the playground told me as we lined up to play basketball.

I answered, confused, "She's not my sister, duh. She's just my friend."

"Well, who cares? You look the same to me," he concluded, as if that were a fair explanation of his assumption that because we both had black hair and dark eyes, we must be related.

There were only a handful of non-Caucasians in the college mountain town where I grew up, and being mistaken for a sister to all other Asians within sight was a frequent occurrence during my childhood. While obviously annoying in some ways, growing up a minority was, in hindsight, also surprisingly beneficial—no one ever told me it was weird or inappropriate that, as a girl, I liked math and science,

click

because I already fit easily into the stereotype of being a nerdy, smart Asian kid.

A shy and self-conscious girl, I didn't enjoy sharing my opinions out loud. Instead I preferred subjects like math and science because the answers rarely required class discussion and were simply right or wrong. I felt that my cultural differences stuck out less with numbers than with words; it was easy for me to hide out with logic, free of interpretation or personal expression that could lead to embarrassment. Since I was used to feeling different because of my ethnicity, it didn't occur to me that it was also different that I, as a girl, liked math and science. In this way, I let my race trump my gender throughout elementary, junior high, and high school.

I applied to a highly selective, innovative, start-up engineering college. During the admissions process they mentioned that one of the goals of the inaugural class was a fify-fifty gender balance. After an on-campus interview weekend with many other potential students, I got in! I thought it was amazing that they chose me out of all those other qualified, smart, diverse people.

Yes, by miracles of miracles the little engineering college that could did accomplish a nearly equal gender balance for my pioneering class of seventy-five people, something unheard of in engineering. The beginning was cool, just meeting and greeting lots of friendly (mostly white) faces. The first month passed quickly with everyone in the class of only seventy-five making first impressions and getting to know each other. Notable characteristics among the students quickly emerged: who raises their hands, who is really slow to understand stuff, who loves to hear themselves talk, who brought a rice cooker, who likes basketball, and of course, who is "smart."

During that first month, everyone was figuring out where they fit in and questioning how they got there in the first place. Students started talking/reasoning/slippery sloping about the admissions process, asking out loud and publicly: "Exactly how did the college achieve this fify-fifty gender balance when more men applied than women? . . . That must mean that it was easier for women to get in than men, that they were given preferential treatment. . . . That must mean that some women were given their spots just because they were women. . . . That must mean there are women here who aren't as qualified as some of the male applicants and, consequently, don't deserve it! . . . AND, that must mean that the women, on average, are stupider than the men and don't belong here—they shouldn't be here!"

Since I was initially very surprised that I had been admitted to this prestigious institution, this runaway train of bad conclusions ran me over, preying on my inexperience in being summarily judged as a female. Unlike high school, where my race helped me fit in as a stereotypical nerdy Asian doing math and science, it now seemed to make my situation even worse— as both a minority and a female, I counted doubly for the diversity of the college, a stated goal of the admissions process. So I had to wonder, was checking the boxes for "female" and "Asian/Pacific Islander" what got me in? Did I not deserve to be here by my own merit?

I had previously found solace in the unbiased, impartial nature of math and statistics but now had difficulty reassuring myself using the numbers. How could a heavily male applicant pool equal a gender-balanced incoming class? That equation did not have any purely logical solution. There had to be another factor at play, some variable I had not considered and did not understand.

To make matters worse, some of my classmates felt compelled to make a list of the ten smartest students in the class. Looking back, this insidious list was the result of awkward eighteen-year-olds who were formerly the smartest fish in their high school ponds, now swimming into a new school and trying to understand where they fit in. Not surprising, the list was dominated by men who volunteered their opinions all the time in class, naturally responded to questions with authority, and easily stated things in tones that really meant "I know the answer, and it is trivially obvious to someone with brainpower as superior as mine."

Missing from the list, of course, were the meek ones: students who knew all of the answers but didn't need to broadcast them and, like me, students who sometimes had correct answers but stated them with uncertainty instead of condescending self-assuredness. I had more respect for the people who didn't need to announce their intelligence to everyone else, yet "the list" seemed to indicate that to be considered smart, you had to be the type to let everyone know—a type that was overwhelmingly male.

I knew that the people making these lists and starting rumors about the admissions process were being completely baseless assholes. We all had different means of "belonging" in the small community of seventy-five people, but if this start-up college was to be a success, we had to be in it together, dammit! I wanted to be able to tell them to shut up with absolute factual (and not-too-emotional) certainty. I needed to understand, for myself, how the system actually worked—did I really get extra points for being an Asian woman? Were the men really more qualified and generally smarter than the women? Why did people seem to think so? The need to answer these questions marked the beginning of my journey into feminism.

I went to the dean of student life and the dean of admissions and asked each of them, point-blank, if the admitted women were less qualified than the men, if there was purposeful bias in the admissions procedure. They both told me the same story:

Female applicants tend to be more self-selecting than the males in several ways. Women who do not think they will get in do not apply, whereas men are more likely to apply regardless of their level of preparation/qualification. Moreover, women who are interested in engineering have already made a personal choice. Rarely pushed into math and science fields, the women who are interested in engineering already have legitimate self-engagement—whereas for males, some apply to engineering school because of recommendations from guidance counselors or parents. Consequently, the quality of the women applicants is, as a whole, higher than the quality of the male applicants. Despite the discrepancy in the sheer numbers of applications, those accepted are of equal quality and, of course, equally deserving of being enrolled at the college.

Was it really a satisfactory explanation? I was reassured by their soft reasoning but had to wonder if their argument really explained what was going on. There was a lot more to the story than just the numbers of male and female applicants; there were real differences in the treatment and approach to math, science, and engineering careers for men and women, and the consequences of those differences were evident in my very own class. I could no longer trust the numbers to tell the full story; I could no longer ignore that there were structural and institutional factors that encouraged and celebrated men in technical fields but simultaneously dissuaded and ignored women. The missing variable in the admissions equation was how each of us had been individually socialized: Every one of our personal experiences shaped the path to our current destination at school, and on the whole, these experiences were particularly different between men and women.

I started to consider—how deep did this go? Every equation or law we were learning in class had a man's name attached to it: Isaac Newton's laws, James Maxwell's equations, the calculus of Gottfried Leibniz, James Watson and Francis Crick's DNA helix . . . yes, the list of equations named after (white) male names felt endless. Growing up I had been reassured by the unbiased nature of math and science, yet in my college education, all I could see were male names getting all the glory. Was

click

this also an indication that somehow men were naturally better at making scientific discoveries, or was it just like the smart list? Were these men just better at publicizing their knowledge? Would this ever get better? Beginning to feel truly discouraged for the first time, I realized that it was situations like these that reinforced society's prejudices and assumptions, feeding into the spiraling feedback loop discouraging women in science, math, and engineering.

During my junior year, I decided to do research with a physics professor who, in addition to studying physical phenomena in the lab, was also interested in engineering education. Her project looked at how teaching students with hands-on projects instead of lectures affected the way the students, particularly women, responded to the subjects of math, science, and engineering. It was my job to transcribe, read, and tag relevant sections of one-on-one interviews a neutral party had conducted with male and female engineering students about their experiences both inside and outside the classroom during their first semesters on our campus.

To my amazement, while listening and reading through multitudes of these interviews I found several people whose stories mirrored mine closely—others who had experienced the same self-doubts after classmates questioned the fairness of the admissions process, others who wondered if they really deserved to be at the school. Ridiculously enough, the interviewees even described the creation of a mostly male smart list during the first semester! The similarity of these stories to my own experiences was striking.

Hearing my worries and concerns repeated by other people convinced me that the questions I was facing were not rare. Now my logical and mathematical mind was thinking statistically: Anything that happened twice in these independent populations was likely to happen again and again unless significant changes were made to convince women that they really were equal, despite the smart lists and stupid rumors of preferential treatment. My desire to prevent these events from reoccurring drove me to be more vocal and outspoken, to make everyone feel welcome in studying engineering, math, and science.

I began to read and discuss more—first about gender differences in the sciences and gradually more about feminism. Previously, when I thought that adhering to the smart Asian stereotype protected me from being judged as a female, I had been covering my eyes and limiting what I could see. Now I understood that there was no hiding from the real world and the real prejudices that do exist, and I finally took the blinders off. With the full imperfect picture in sight I had a clear goal— to keep others from falling into the same holes I had in doubting my own abilities because I was a woman—and in accepting that goal I also accepted my role to create change as a feminist.

∽☙∼

I Was an Obnoxious Teenage Feminist

Jessica Valenti

⌒

The first time I went to Washington DC was in 1992, and I was with my mother. She kept insisting that I take pictures in front of various landmarks and museums. If you look at the pictures now, you'll see me at thirteen years old—a hunched over, sullen teen giving my mother the look of death. I was a pretty obnoxious kid; I didn't want to go sightseeing, and I certainly didn't want to be seen with my mom. I was too cool for that sort of thing. (But not too cool, apparently, for Dwayne Wayne sunglasses.) Besides, we weren't there to pose in front of the Washington Monument; we were there for a pro-choice march—a march that would turn out to be hundreds of thousands of women strong.

I had to convince my mom—through numerous fights and debates—that a thirteen-year-old was perfectly capable of deciding she wanted to go to a protest. My mother's concern was that she was pushing her pro-choice beliefs onto me before I was old enough to decide for myself. With an eye-roll and a huff I explained that I was *already* pro-choice and it *certainly* had nothing to do with her. My mom eventually relented, and I got to travel to DC for what would be the defining moment in my feminist awakening. (Of course at the time I was more concerned about what I would wear and how I could avoid looking like I was with my mom in public places. Charming, I know.)

Despite all of the trouble I went through to be able to go to the DC march for reproductive rights, I didn't call myself a feminist. I don't know that I ever even *thought* about it. I knew that I believed in the right to abortion, I was all too aware of sexism, and I was a superopinionated, loud teenager. Yet identifying as a feminist never occurred to me.

But no matter the reason, that all was about to change.

After all of the requisite tourist stuff, the day of the march arrived. I was more nervous than I wanted to let on; I wasn't sure what to expect. I figured a protest would mean lots of angry women, lots of signs, and yelling and screaming. (And while I could talk a good game in class or among my friends, yelling in public seemed overwhelming.) Well . . . I was right about the signs.

What I saw blew me away—all of these women, thousands of women, all smiling and joyful. *That* I wasn't prepared for—the joy. Everyone at the march was just happy to be with each other. The people we marched next to introduced themselves to us. Other women gave out bottles of water and buttons to those who didn't have them. And yes, some people were yelling, but they had smiles on as they did so. I got carried away in the moment and even forgot for a second that I was supposed to be irritable that my mom was linking arms with me.

There was a dark moment, however—one that's still vivid in my mind, even all of these years later. On the sidelines of the protest stood dozens of anti-choice counterprotesters. They were decidedly *not* joyful. They were screaming at us, calling us—calling me!—murderers. Most of them were men. One man was dressed as the grim reaper—he wore a skull mask on his face and had a scythe in one hand. In his other hand he had a baby doll covered in blood; he was holding it upside down by its feet. It was simply terrifying. Looking at him, and then at the kind faces surrounding me—it was never clearer what "side" I wanted to be on.

I was so moved by the march, I couldn't help but lose a little of my adolescent sassiness. The pictures from the march show me smiling (unheard of in those days!) and laughing with my mother. That's the kind of person I wanted—and still want—to be.

When I returned to school, my humanities teacher encouraged me to talk about the march to my eighth-grade class. I felt important, being able to relay my experience and having the class debate about abortion. And even though some people disagreed with me, a lot didn't—and everyone was excited to hear about what went down in DC. It was one of the first moments I had speaking my mind, feeling informed, when I realized that this was something I could do: I could argue passionately—and really well!

It was this series of events—the march and then representing my beliefs in class—that made me a feminist. I was probably a feminist prior to these experiences through my beliefs and general loudmouthness. I still wasn't even calling myself a feminist. But there was something that happened at that march, and after, that made me realize that I wanted to do something with my life that contributed to the joy that I saw that day, and the pride I felt in class.

When I think back now, it's hard to believe what a little snot I was to my mom (something I've long since apologized for, believe me). After all, she was the one who had taught me

click

to speak my mind and that girls could do anything boys could do. She is the reason I am who I am. Ironically, it was also her strength that spelled my reticence to the feminist label. It was all just too scary. To call myself a feminist was to identify with my mother.

Part of getting older is owning the facets of your identity that frighten you the most; click moments are the wonderful instances where you can *feel* yourself growing up. And I can think of nothing better to grow up into than a feminist.

✧

PILLOW DANCING AND OTHER FAILED HETERO EXPERIMENTS

Miriam Zoila Pérez

———

After a big family dinner, my dad and stepmom were settled into the couch, watching *Crossfire*—a favorite conservative political show of Pop's (my brother and I call him Pop, short for *papi*). Fourteen and full of angst, I walked into the living room and blurted out: "But what if *I* got pregnant?" I was still burning up from our debate during dinner about teen pregnancy. "You wouldn't get pregnant, first of all, but if you did," Pop stated definitively, "I think you should be sent away as a punishment."

This was not an atypical exchange for us. You name a political wedge issue, and we probably debated it. His challenges and talking points taught me how to hone my arguments and make them as opposition-ready as possible. Want to talk about abortion? I could run down the list of typical anti-choice arguments and come up with my standard responses. Want to debate about biological differences between the sexes? I had a retort for all the standard challenges—what about sports? Muscle definition? Intelligence?

It's not easy for me to admit that conversations with my conservative father, most of which put him on the decidedly antifeminist side of things, were a large part of my feminist formation. While I no longer have the patience for these kinds of debates with Pop, I do have to give him credit for always making me feel respected during our back-and-forths. Just the fact that he was willing to engage with me, beginning as early as eleven or twelve years old, showed me that my ideas did matter, regardless of how wrong he thought I was.

I wish I could point to a day when one of these arguments really crystallized my feminist identity. I wish I could say that one night, over arroz con pollo, I declared to my family around the table—"I'm a feminist!" Unfortunately I can't, and that's because I didn't come to feminism in any one single moment. I pretty much rejected the term for a long time, afraid of the connotations that came with it, not wanting to differentiate myself from my peers. But long before I embraced the term, my experiences slowly shaped my feminist perspective.

I grew up in a Southern college town. My parents are Cuban exiles who left the island in the 1960s during the first wave of emigration after the Cuban Revolution. While many people believe that all Cuban Americans are conservative, my mom is in fact quite liberal—a sharp distinction from my father. They divorced when I was four, so a relatively apolitical atmosphere at my mom's house tempered my experiences with contentious political discussions over dinner at my father's.

While Pop and I debated every political issue under the sun, the one that was always a recurring theme for us was gender roles. I pushed against the idea that boys were inherently different from girls, and he pushed right back. He even bought me a book for my seventeenth birthday, *Why Sex Matters: A Darwinian Look at Human Behavior,* as a response to my constant questioning of the gender binary and its links to biology. He was an unfailing gender essentialist, attributing everything to biology and the influences of evolution. I just couldn't accept his arguments about cavemen, hunter-gatherers, and their ties to inherent male aggression.

I didn't only explore these questions about gender roles by debating with Pop. My friends and I spent the majority of our social lives through high school trying to perfect the art of relating to and understanding boys. From a really young age (I had my first "boyfriend" in first grade), boys were all I talked about with my circle of friends—boys were our world. From elementary school until the day I graduated high school, dating boys was what we did, talked about, and breathed.

When we were young it was pretty innocent. Take for example my third-grade boyfriend William. He and I only had one face-to-face conversation during the entirety of our relationship before I decided it was time to end things. I used the 1990s version of the text message breakup, avoiding any direct contact with him, by asking my friend to tell his friend to tell him it was over. This was standard practice; my friends and I went through multiple boyfriends this way, and it kept things feeling light and inconsequential.

As we reached middle school, things turned slightly more racy, and stories of friends "hitting the bases" with their boyfriends were common. Actual sex was still rare, but the other bases (French, feel, finger—the four Fs we called them) were fair game. I was really into hearing about my friends' escapades even though my streak with boys ended after it was no longer acceptable to ask someone out using the telephone game.

If I look back at my journals from those years, it's incredible to believe I was ever so boy focused. Crush after crush written about extensively and in excruciating detail. I even had

two poems published in an early Chicken Soup for the Teenage Soul spin-off called *Teen Love: On Relationships*. One poem
pretty much sums up how I was feeling during those years: "I
wonder, / What I could do / Or say / To make him like me. / I
wonder, / What or who / I need to be / To be his. / I wonder, /
When just being me / Will be enough."

Each day there was a new object of my affection. Entries
about who danced with whom at the middle school dance,
complete with a full report of the twenty-girl sleepover at
Catherine's house afterward. I remember one such night
clearly, because after not being asked to slow dance at all (I
usually spent those songs consoling some crying friend in the
girls bathroom), I initiated a new game: dancing with pillows.
After making up a dance to Montell Jordan's "This Is How We
Do It," ten of us grabbed pillows from the living room couch
and slow danced with them, pretending they were our imaginary boyfriends.

I didn't see much more action than that pillow dancing for
the rest of middle and most of high school. I like to joke that I
peaked early with boys—I had more boyfriends before the fifth
grade than the rest of my dating career combined. It wasn't
for a lack of trying, that's for sure. I was the girl who the boys
never liked (at least not in *that* way). Friends would all exclaim
that they couldn't possibly understand why. *They* all liked me
so much, they'd tell me after yet another rejection by one of
my crushes.

When I met Lee on a youth group ski trip my junior year
of high school, he didn't have to do much to win my attention. The fact that we shared a bus seat was more coinci-
dence than chemistry, but before I knew it, we were quietly
and sweatily groping one another on the bus ride home as
our friends and a whole crew of Girl Scouts slept soundly
around us. I was young and he was younger, and despite
years of sleepovers spent talking about this exact moment,

I had no idea what I wanted. Still, the simple fact of a boy expressing interest in me was enough to have me giddily sharing the story of our bus seat escapades with my friends the next day during assembly.

Our relationship ended, appropriately, on Friday the thirteenth. It was a stellar day for me, as I had already rear-ended someone in my three-month-old Honda Civic and lost my ATM card before Lee called with the bad news. He needed out, again, and the only good thing was that this time it would be the last. We had spent that summer in limbo—together, not together, but all the while having a lot of not-so-great sex. After I continued to say no to his attempts at getting back together throughout that fall of my senior year, I finally reflected back on our relationship and realized that our sex had not really been consensual. He didn't force me, exactly, but he definitely took advantage of my ill-defined boundaries. I entered into an overly sexual relationship way before I was ready.

During all those sleepovers and discussions about when we should lose the big V, we never decided how we would draw boundaries with our boyfriends or how we would stand strong in the face of persistent challenges to those lines. I certainly never answered the question "What will your first time be like?" with the response: "Oh, I'll be with my not-really boyfriend in the back seat of my car, parked in an abandoned church parking lot using a condom from a gas station dispenser."

So where had I gone wrong? Sadly I wasn't the only one to find myself in this predicament. One by one, most of my friends had similar stories, although the details were slightly different. A couple of my friends had lost their virginity on the eve of the millennium at a house party. They weren't dating those boys either, but they thought it was a good way to celebrate the end of the twentieth century. Another was essentially date-raped at a party she threw while her parents were out of town. None of my friends had the picture perfect first time we had dreamed of and read about in books like Judy Blume's *Forever*.

That last year of high school was probably the most formative for my feminism, even though I was still avoiding using the f-word. I was angry. I was disillusioned. I wanted to know why most of my friends were making the mistakes I had made with boys. Theoretically we had been on the right path to the perfect relationships and perfect first sexual experiences. I thought that all those years of sleepovers and phone conversations would have prepared my friends and me for that first big moment. But for the majority of us, those experiences were coerced or just unsatisfying.

Part of what I began to realize in those months was how much we were all affected by self-esteem, the power dynamics of our interactions with boys, and gendered expectations. Our shared self-esteem issues were not just from unrequited attraction but also from society around us. The personal really did become political when I realized that there were certain things we didn't have control over, no matter how much we wanted things to be different for us. It wasn't as simple as being victims to overly zealous boys. The reality is many of them didn't want to be having sex either—at least I'm pretty sure Lee didn't—but that was what they had been taught to do. Girls were supposed to be the boundary setters, boys were supposed to try and rush to the goal line every time. It was the gendered societal expectations that shaped our experiences, and this connected back to all my debating with my dad about gender difference.

It wasn't easy to be part of my high school social world with these realizations, and my senior year was pretty alienating as a result. My friends didn't like my cynicism, or criticism of our boy-obsessed lives, and often would tell me I was being too feminist. My two closest friends that year even told me I was bringing them down and started excluding me because of it.

Spring break of my freshman year of college in Pennsylvania, I was riding shotgun for one of my Ultimate Frisbee teammates to keep her awake while everyone else slept in the back. I didn't really know much about her—she was new to the team as well, but Dana ended up being one of my most important college friends. When we first met, I assumed she was gay—it was probably the boyish clothing, baseball caps, and short hair that tipped me off. I learned during that van ride that she didn't identify that way and had spent most of her childhood fighting the assumption that she was a lesbian. We quickly became close friends, and I wholly admired and looked up to her for reasons I didn't fully understand until a few years later.

We both ended up coming out around the same time during the spring of our junior year. What I had been really lacking all those years growing up in North Carolina was a model for who I wanted to be—specifically how I wanted to present myself gender-wise. I had spent so many years mimicking my high school friends in both presentation and action that I didn't realize how badly all this suited me until I was exposed to other options. Dana was the first of a number of gender-nonconforming women who would become my role models and give me those examples I had been so lacking. This was all part of my coming out process; I couldn't really start thinking about who I wanted to be with until I knew what I wanted to be like.

All those experiences growing up were fundamentally about pushing at the way gender roles were shaping my life and the lives of the people around me. I constantly argued about these limitations with my dad—why did girls' sports have different rules than boys' sports? I questioned what my friends and I were doing with the boys in the back seats of our cars—why was it so different from what we said we wanted? It wasn't until later that I found support for this

click

questioning through the feminist community on my college campus and beyond. I no longer feel alone in these critiques. I benefit from a community of people who share a similar desire to break down the gender categories that limit us and who question the structures that promote stereotypes. I won't argue with my dad about politics anymore, and I'm miles from those high school back seat moments, but I know they've landed me here. For that I am grateful.

∽◎∽

CONTRIBUTORS

Elisa Albert is the author of *The Book of Dahlia*, a novel, and *How This Night Is Different*, a collection of short stories, and the editor of *Freud's Blind Spot*, an anthology of original essays on siblings. She sometimes teaches creative writing at Columbia University and occasionally lives in scenic Albany, New York, always with the writer Edward Schwarzschild and their wee boy, Miller D. She is currently writer-in-residence at the Netherlands Institute for Advanced Study in Holland.

Jennifer Baumgardner is the coauthor of *Manifesta* and *Grassroots*, the author of *Abortion & Life* and *Look Both Ways*, and the creator of the I Had an Abortion Project and film. She writes frequently for magazines from *Glamour* to *The Nation* to *The Advocate* and teaches writing at the New School. Originally from Fargo, North Dakota, she now lives happily in New York City with her two sons, boyfriend, and step-cat.

Nellie Beckett is an eighteen-year-old writer, editor, poet, performer, cultural critic, and aspiring professional feminist from Silver Spring, Maryland. Her writing has been published

click

in *The Washington Post* and in her high school's award-winning newspaper, *Silver Chips*, of which she is editor in chief. Read more of her work at thefbomb.org.

Jordan Berg Powers is an organizer, political consultant, and freelance writer in Worcester, Massachusetts. His work reflects the political activism that has shaped his adult life, and he frequently gives talks on media, hip-hop, social justice, Judaism, international politics, and the role of men in feminism. Recently, he has been a guest lecturer/presenter at the Women, Action and Media Conference, the Hip Hop Congress National Convention, Smith College, and the University of Massachusetts Amherst. Jordan has a master's in international politics from the London School of Oriental & African Studies and bachelor's degrees in international development and economics from American University. His writing can be found at his blog, www.blackjew.net. He is currently working on two manuscripts: one fiction, and one a practical guide to understanding our failed media system.

Elizabeth Chiles Shelburne is a Tennessee girl at heart, even though she has suffered through twelve (and counting) Massachusetts winters. When she's not on blues-and-barbeque road trips through the South or riding four-wheelers through the African bush, she sits at her kitchen table and writes. She has been the grateful recipient of an International Reporting Project fellowship and a Kaiser Family Foundation fellowship that have allowed her to travel to Uganda and South Africa, where she reported on global health stories. She has written for *The Atlantic Monthly*, *Globalpost*, *The Boston Globe*, and *Boston Magazine*, among others. She lives outside Boston with her husband and is at work on her first novel.

Li Sydney Cornfeld writes theater criticism at Offoffonline and dispenses etiquette guidance through Etiqast, currently in production. She has a bachelor's degree from Vassar College and is pursuing a master's in performance studies at New York University. Originally from Saint Louis, she lives in Brooklyn with wonderful roommates and Emma Goldman, a goldfish.

Born and raised in Detroit, **Anitra Cottledge** left that part of the Midwest to pursue her education in . . . another part of the Midwest. She earned her master's from the University of Minnesota in educational policy and administration, with a re-search focus on women of color in higher education administra-tive leadership. As the assistant director of a campus women's center, Cottledge is both professionally and personally invested in addressing the intersections of race, gender, class, and other identities. She gets fired up and will happily take up conversa-tions with anyone about why we still need campus women's centers, why even the most dedicated activists need to go home at the end of the day, and why feminism is everybody's issue. In her free time, she reads and writes voraciously, researches her family tree, and dreams of taking salsa lessons.

Marni Grossman holds a bachelor's degree from Vassar in women's studies. The degree turned out to be of little practical value but nonetheless holds a lot of sentimental weight. She's written for *Heeb*, *Sadie Magazine*, *BUST*, *Playgirl*, and *gURL. com*. Her interests include subverting the patriarchy, reading, and *Law and Order:* the Jerry Orbach years. She'd like to know why the inhabitants of the tiny Maine hamlet Cabot Cove so frequently come to violent ends. She'd also like someone to hire her. You can read more of her writing at thenervousbreak down.com.

click

Shelby Knox is nationally known as the subject of the Sundance-award-winning film *The Education of Shelby Knox*, a 2005 documentary chronicling her teenage activism for comprehensive sex education and gay rights in her Southern Baptist community. After the film's release, Shelby became a national advocate for comprehensive sex education, testifying before city councils, state legislatures, and the Ways and Means Committee of the House of Representatives about the failure of abstinence-only-until-marriage programs. She has appeared on *The Today Show*, *The Daily Show*, and *Hardball* and sat down with both Dr. Phil and Al Franken to discuss sex education and her virginity. She continues to travel the country as an itinerant feminist organizer, doing trainings, workshops, and civil disobedience in the name of reproductive justice and sexual health. Shelby lives in New York City, where she spends her days in cafés trying to finish a book on the next generation of feminist activism.

Colleen Lutz Clemens, PhD, has worked with students in a variety of settings, from public high schools to private universities. Her research interests focus on women's studies and postcolonial literatures of Southeast Asia, Africa, and the Middle East. She currently teaches writing and postcolonial literature courses and is working on a book that focuses on the politics of Islamic veiling practices in literary texts. As Lehigh University's Global Citizenship Teaching Fellow for two years, she had the opportunity to accompany students to South Africa and India. In her spare time, she travels to France; plays with her dog; enjoys the scenery of Bucks County, Pennsylvania, from the back of her husband's motorcycle; and writes poetry and essays.

Jillian Mackenzie has worked as an editor and writer at *Allure*, *Seventeen*, *Cosmopolitan*, and *Self* magazines. She lives with her boyfriend and their two cats in New York City.

Courtney E. Martin is a writer living in Brooklyn. Her next book, *Do It Anyway: The Next Generation of Teachers, Advocates, and Activists*, will be published in fall 2010 by Beacon Press. Her first book, *Perfect Girls, Starving Daughters: How the Quest for Perfection Is Harming Young Women*, was critically acclaimed and called "a hardcover punch in the gut" by Arianna Huffington. She is also an editor for Feministing and a frequent commentator on television, including *The O'Reilly Factor*, *The Today Show*, and *Good Morning America*. Courtney is a senior correspondent for The American Prospect Online, and her work has appeared in *The Washington Post, Newsweek,* and *The Christian Science Monitor*, among others. Courtney cowrote the life story of AIDS activist Marvelyn Brown, called *The Naked Truth: Young, Beautiful and (HIV) Positive*. She was awarded the Elie Wiesel Prize in Ethics in 2002 and is the youngest woman to ever be awarded a residency at the Rockefeller Foundation's Bellagio Center in Italy. She is the founder of the Secret Society for Creative Philanthropy and always interested in being a part of unself-conscious dance parties, just FYI. Read more about her work at www.courtneyemartin.com.

Winter Miller is a playwright and periodic journalist. Or vice versa. The two collided when she wrote a play about genocide and traveled to Darfur with her boss and mentor, journalist Nicholas Kristof. *In Darfur* premiered at The Public Theater followed by a standing-room-only performance at their eighteen-hundred-seat theater in Central Park, a first for a play by a woman. Among Winter's plays, some have been published and performed in London, Uganda, and North America. Others are flammable. As a journalist, Winter once chased a tornado and spent a week at Graceland, although not simultaneously. She has written for *The New York Times, Variety, New York Magazine,* and *The Boston*

Globe. Winter has an MFA in playwriting from Columbia University and graduated cum laude from Smith College. She is a proud member of 13Playwrights. Her first job out of college was as an NBC page. She kept her uniform.

Olessa Pindak is the Deputy Editor of Health and Beauty at *Body + Soul* magazine and also covers beauty and health for *Martha Stewart Living.* She's worked in magazines for nine years at publications such as *Allure, Natural Health,* and *Fit Pregnancy.* Olessa lives and works in New York City.

Karen Pittelman is the author of *Classified: How to Stop Hiding Your Privilege and Use It for Social Change* and coauthor of *Creating Change Through Family Philanthropy,* both from Soft Skull Press and written for the nonprofit organization Resource Generation. She served as Resource Generation's first program coordinator, working to organize young people with wealth who believe in social justice. In 2000, she dissolved her $3 million trust fund to cofound the Chahara Foundation, a fund run by and for low-income women activists in Boston. She currently works as a writing coach in New York City.

Sophie Pollitt-Cohen currently writes humor pieces for *History Magazine* and *The Huffington Post.* She is coauthor of the bestselling book *The Notebook Girls.* Sophie graduated from Wesleyan University in 2009. She's into Ben Franklin, pie, and leather leggings.

Alissa Quart is an author and journalist. Her latest book on alternative culture is forthcoming from Farrar, Straus, and Giroux. She is also the author of the books *Hothouse Kids* and *Branded* and writes a column for *Columbia Journalism Review,* where she is a contributing editor. She has written for *The New York Times Magazine*, *Newsweek*, and many other places and is an adjunct professor at Columbia University Graduate School of Journalism. In 2009 and 2010, she was a Nieman Fellow at Harvard University.

Amy Richards is the author of *Opting In: Having a Child Without Losing Yourself* and the coauthor (with Jennifer Baumgardner) of *Manifesta: Young Women, Feminism & the Future* and *Grassroots: A Field Guide to Feminist Activism*. Amy is also a cofounder of the Third Wave Foundation and the voice behind Ask Amy, an online advice column at www.feminist.com.

Marta L. Sanchez is a self-taught visual artist, writer, and activist who uses her work to address sexual violence. She has traveled with her unique combination of personal storytelling, visual art, and spoken word to colleges, universities, conferences, and community centers as far away as Croatia. She loves chocolate, floating in the ocean, and envisioning a safer world, one brushstroke at a time. For more information, visit her website: www.poetryandart.org.

Joshunda Sanders is a reporter for the Austin American-Statesman in Austin, Texas. She has also written for the *Houston Chronicle*, *Beaumont Enterprise*, *Seattle Post-Intelligencer*, and *San Francisco Chronicle*. Her essays have appeared in *Secrets and Confidences: The Complicated Truth about Women's Friendships*, *Homelands*, and most recently, *P.S. What I Didn't Say* (Seal Press). She graduated from Vassar College in 2000, where she majored in creative writing. In 2009, she earned a master's of science and information studies from the University of Texas.

click

Rachel Shukert is the author of the books *Have You No Shame?* and *Everything Is Going to be Great*. Her work has appeared in numerous anthologies and publications, such as *McSweeney's*, *Salon*, *Nerve*, and *The Daily Beast*, among many others. She is also a playwright and poet. Rachel was raised in Omaha, Nebraska, and lives in New York City.

Deborah Siegel, PhD, is an expert on gender, politics, and the unfinished business of feminism across generations. She is the author of *Sisterhood, Interrupted: From Radical Women to Grrls Gone Wild*, coeditor of the literary anthology *Only Child: Writers on the Singular Joys and Solitary Sorrows of Growing Up Solo*, founder of the blog Girl w/Pen, and cofounder of the webjournal *The Scholar & Feminist Online*. Deborah is currently working on a book about how feminism has—and hasn't—changed men. Her writings have appeared in venues including *The Washington Post*, *The Guardian*, *Slate's The Big Money*, *Recessionwire*, *The Huffington Post*, *The American Prospect*, *More*, *Psychology Today*, and *The Mothers Movement Online*. She is a graduate of the Women's Media Center's Progressive Women's Voices program, a Fellow at the Woodhull Institute, and a board member of the Council on Contemporary Families. She is currently vice president of education at SheWrites.

Amy Spalding lives in Los Angeles, where she works in advertising and writes young adult novels. She attended Webster University and is currently studying gender as portrayed on television at the New School. Visit her at www.theamyspalding.com.

Mathangi Subramanian is an Indian American writer and educator. She is currently assistant director of International Education and Research at Sesame Workshop, the nonprofit that produces *Sesame Street*. She earned her doctorate in education from Columbia Teachers College, where she wrote her dissertation on the ways in which South Asian American teenage women use the Internet to stay connected to their ethnic identity. Her children's fiction has appeared in *Kahani*, and her scholarly work has appeared in *Penn GSE Perspectives on Urban Education*, *Current Issues in Comparative Education*, and the *Encyclopedia of Women and Islamic Cultures*. She currently lives in New York City with her pet rabbit, Nova, who shares her love of crunchy vegetables and afternoon naps. She is nobody's wife and nobody's mother.

J. Courtney Sullivan is the author of the best-selling novel *Commencement*, about which Gloria Steinem wrote, "generous-hearted, brave . . . *Commencement* makes clear that the feminist revolution is just beginning." Courtney is a Brooklyn-based writer whose work has appeared in *The New York Times*, *New York Magazine*, *Elle*, *Glamour*, *Cosmopolitan*, *Allure*, *In Style*, *Men's Vogue*, the *New York Observer*, *Tango*, and in the essay anthology *The Secret Currency of Love*. She also contributes to the website someecards.com. Courtney is a graduate of Smith College, works in the editorial department of *The New York Times*, and serves on the advisory board of Girls Write Now. Read more about her at www.jcourtneysullivan.com.

Rebecca Traister is a senior writer at Salon.com, where she covers women in politics, media, and entertainment. She has also written for *The New York Observer*, *Elle*, *The Nation*, *The New York Times*, and *Glamour*. She is at work on a book about women and the 2008 presidential election called *Big Girls Don't Cry* that is scheduled to be published in 2010.

click

Janet Tsai resides in Boulder, Colorado, where she is figuring
out how to be an engineer while still maintaining her sanity
and identity. Previously a China-based manufacturing liaison
and a usability specialist, designer, and systems engineer for
the Roomba robotic vacuum cleaner, Janet is now nurturing
broader interests in consumer products and how to create items
that women will really want to use. She is also exploring ways
to make engineering, math, and science more appealing to the
female youth of America; pondering a mash-up of yoga with
physics; and thinking about the creation of teaching examples
that do not involve planes, trains, or automobiles. Janet holds a
bachelor's degree in mechanical engineering from Olin College
and is a registered yoga therapist. In her spare time, Janet cooks
and devours mad amounts of Chinese food, reads romance and
science fiction, hikes the beautiful Rocky Mountains, and rants
about the ongoing consequences of the male legacy in engineering.

Jessica Valenti is a feminist writer and blogger. She is the
founder and editor of the popular blog and online community
Feministing.com and the author of three books: *Full Frontal
Feminism: A Young Woman's Guide to Why Feminism Matters*;
*He's a Stud, She's a Slut . . . and 49 Other Double Standards Ev-
ery Woman Should Know*; and *The Purity Myth: How America's
Obsession with Virginity Is Hurting Young Women*. She is also
a coeditor of the anthology *Yes Means Yes: Visions of Female
Sexual Power and a World Without Rape*. Jessica's writing has
appeared in *The Nation, The Guardian* (UK), *The American
Prospect, Ms.,* Salon.com, and *Bitch*. She received her master's
degree in women's and gender studies from Rutgers University,
where she is now a part-time lecturer. Jessica speaks at universities and organizations across the country on feminism, blog-
ging, and politics.

Miriam Zoila Pérez is a twenty-five-year-old writer, blogger, and reproductive justice activist. Miriam has worked as an organizer and advocate for Latina women in various capacities, including with the National Latina Institute for Reproductive Health. She is a trained doula, and the sole blogger and founder of radicaldoula.com. She is also an editor at Feministing.com, and her writing has appeared in numerous online and print publications, including the recent anthology *Yes Means Yes: Visions of Female Sexual Power and a World without Rape*. Miriam is a member of the board of directors of the Sistersong Women of Color Reproductive Health Collective and the Astraea Lesbian Foundation for Justice. She lives in Washington DC.

ACKNOWLEDGMENTS

The Courtneys would like to thank both the rabble-rousing feminists who preceded us—especially our mentors and mamas—and the crew of amazing young feminist friends and colleagues who we email in the middle of the day when misogynistic bullshit gets us down.

We would also like to thank Courtney S.'s wonderful agent, Brettne Bloom at Kneerim and Williams; editor extraordinaire Krista Lyons for instantly understanding why this book was necessary; and everyone at Seal Press.

Thanks most of all to our amazing contributors—their words, wit, and wisdom prove that feminism is most certainly not dead. In fact, it's alive and well. It's thriving in the most unlikely places. It often possesses a wicked sort of humor and a kick-ass fashion sense. Sometimes even fishnets.

Oh, and finally, thanks Courtney. No Courtney, thank you.

SELECTED TITLES FROM SEAL PRESS

For more than thirty years, Seal Press has published groundbreaking books. By women. For women. Visit our website at www.sealpress.com. Check out the Seal Press blog at www.sealpress.com/blog.

Girldrive: Criss-Crossing America, Redefining Feminism, by Nona Willis Aronowitz and Emma Bee Bernstein. $19.95, 978-1-58005-273-3. Two young women set out on the open road to explore the current state of feminism in the U.S.

Get Opinionated: A Progressive's Guide to Finding Your Voice (and Taking A Little Action), by Amanda Marcotte. $15.95, 978-1-58005-302-0. Hilarious, bold, and very opinionated, this book helps young women get a handle on the issues they care about—and provides suggestions for the small steps they can take towards change.

Full Frontal Feminism: A Young Woman's Guide to Why Feminism Matters, by Jessica Valenti. $15.95, 978-1-58005-201-6. A sassy and in-your-face look at contemporary feminism for women of all ages.

Listen Up: Voices from the Next Feminist Generation, edited by Barbara Findlen. $16.95, 978-1-58005-054-8. A collection of essays featuring the voices of today's young feminists on racism, sexuality, identity, AIDS, revolution, abortion, and much more.

Colonize This!: Young Women of Color on Today's Feminism, edited by Daisy Hernandez and Bushra Rehman. $16.95, 978-1-58005-067-8. An insight into a new generation of brilliant, outspoken women of color—how they are speaking to the concerns of a new feminism, and their place in it.

It's a Jungle Out There: The Feminist Survival Guide to Politically Inhospitable Environments, by Amanda Marcotte. $13.95, 978-1-58005-226-9. All the witty comebacks, in-your-face retorts, and priceless advice women need to survive in politically hostile environments.